LOW-FAT
PASTA

LOW-FAT PASTA

hamlyn

Published in the UK in 1997
by Hamlyn, a division of Octopus Publishing Group Ltd
2–4 Heron Quays, London E14 4JP

This edition published 2002 by Octopus Publishing Group Ltd

Copyright ©1997, 2002 Octopus Publishing Group Ltd

ISBN 0 600 60824 7

Printed in China

NOTES

Both metric and imperial measurements have been given in
all recipes. Use one set of measurements only and not a
mixture of both.

Standard level spoon measurements are used in all recipes.
1 tablespoon = one 15 ml spoon
1 teaspoon = one 5 ml spoon

Eggs should be medium to large unless otherwise stated.
The Department of Health advises that eggs should not be
consumed raw. This book contains dishes made with raw or
lightly cooked eggs. It is prudent for more vulnerable people
such as pregnant and nursing mothers, invalids, the elderly,
babies and young children to avoid uncooked or lightly cooked
dishes made with eggs. Once prepared, these dishes should
be kept refrigerated and used promptly.
Milk should be full fat unless otherwise stated.

Meat and poultry should be cooked thoroughly. To test if
poultry is cooked, pierce the flesh through the thickest part
with a skewer or fork – the juices should run clear, never pink
or red. Do not re-freeze poultry that has been frozen
previously and thawed.

Do not re-freeze a dish that has been frozen previously.

Pepper should be freshly ground black pepper unless
otherwise stated.
Fresh herbs should be used, unless otherwise stated. If
unavailable, use dried herbs as an alternative but halve the
quantities stated.

Measurements for canned food have been given as a standard
metric equivalent.

Nuts and nut derivatives
This book includes dishes made with nuts and nut derivatives.
It is advisable for customers with known allergic reactions to
nuts and nut derivatives and those who may be potentially
vulnerable to these allergies, such as pregnant and nursing
mothers, invalids, the elderly, babies and children, to avoid
dishes made with nuts and nut oils. It is also prudent to
check the labels of pre-prepared ingredients for the possible
inclusion of nut derivatives.

Vegetarians should look for the 'V' symbol on a cheese to
ensure it is made with vegetarian rennet. There are vegetarian
forms of Parmesan, Feta, Cheddar, Cheshire, Red Leicester,
dolcelatte and many goats' cheeses, among others.
* indicates recipe contains fish, unsuitable for vegans.

Ovens should be preheated to the specified temperature –
if using a fan-assisted oven, follow the manufacturer's
instructions for adjusting the time and the temperature.

All the recipes in this book have been analysed by a
professional nutritionist, so that you can see their nutritional
content at a glance. The abbreviations are as follows:
Kcal = calories; KJ = kilojoules; CHO = carbohydrate. The
analysis refers to each portion. Use in conjunction with the
chart on page 6.

Contents

Introduction

We eat very well in the Western world, our daily menu containing lots of meats, rich dairy products and manufactured foods containing significant amounts of sugars and fats, which give them a distinctive flavour and creamy and pleasant texture. Unfortunately, many of us eat too well, taking in much more of these foods, especially fats, than our bodies need for good health and which our rather sedentary, low-exercise way of life does not allow us to burn off, leaving many of us overweight and prone to diseases, especially of the heart and other vital organs.

Fat is one of the three components

of food that provide it with calories (or units of energy), the other two being proteins and carbohydrates. Fat itself comes in two types, saturated and unsaturated. The unsaturated fats group contains two sub-groups, polyunsaturated and monounsaturated fats. The table below shows what proportions of our daily calorie intake should be in the form of these different kinds of fat.

Saturated fats are the fats we should be cutting down on because too much of them causes cholesterol levels in the blood to rise, increasing the incidence of coronary heart disease. The main sources of saturated fats are animal products, such as dairy products and meat, especially red meat,

In general, as a rule of thumb, whatever your daily calorie intake, the recommended proportions of nutrients are as follows:

NUTRIENT	RECOMMENDED INTAKE	NUTRIENT	RECOMMENDED INTAKE
Total fat	35% of total energy (kcal) (e.g. in a 2000 calorie diet not more than 700 calories should come from fat. This equals 80 g fat per day, or 40 g fat for every 1000 calories)	**Monounsaturated fatty acids**	10–15% of total energy (kcal)
Saturated fatty acids	Less than 10% of total energy (kcal)	**Carbohydrate**	50% of total calories
		Protein	10–20% of total calories
Polyunsaturated fatty acids	Up to 10% of total energy (kcal)	**Total calories**	To achieve and maintain desirable weight

and hard fats and margarine and hydrogenated vegetable oils.

Small amounts of polyunsaturated fats which are essential for the maintenance of good health, are found in vegetable oils, including sunflower oil and corn oil, and in oily fish, such as salmon, mackerel, herring, sardines and trout. Sources of monounsaturated fats include avocados and many nuts and nut oils such as groundnut oil.

While we have come to recognize the dangers to health in over-indulging in fats, especially saturated fats, and to accept that although we need a certain amount of fat in our diet we generally need a lot less than we actually eat, and that, without some guidance, it is not that easy to reduce the fat content of our diet.

Low-fat Pasta concentrates on pasta, a food recognized as being an ideal basis for low-fat cooking, and has been carefully planned to ensure that the sauces, meats, vegetables and other foods served with the pasta have no more fat in them than is necessary. Great care has been taken, too, to ensure that all dishes are full of flavour, and that reducing the fat content has not compromised the taste.

PASTA IN LOW-FAT COOKING

Most pastas are, in themselves, low in fat. Most of the plain pastas made from durum wheat semolina, such as spaghetti, tagliatelle, farfalle, penne and other shaped pastas, contain about 1g fat per 100g of pasta. Wholewheat pastas contain more -

about 3g fat per 100g. Egg pasta, the most popular kind of homemade pasta, has about 4g of fat per 100g of pasta. The pasta with the highest fat content is flavoured instant noodles, with 6g or more of fat per 100g.

Delicious in its own right, pasta is a starchy food, ideal for 'filling up on'. It also combines well with a great variety of foods, from vegetables to fish and shellfish, meat and poultry to pulses and herbs. Thus, pasta need not be just a basis for main course dishes, but can be an important ingredient in soups, starters and salads.

COOKING THE LOW-FAT WAY

Cooking pasta by itself requires no fat – just plenty of boiling water and a bit of salt, plus some attention so that it does not become overcooked and soggy. Pasta is cooked when it is *al dente* – that is, firm in the centre when broken between finger and thumb. More thought must go into preparing and cooking the low-fat foods to be served with the pasta. Here are some useful tips:

• Use good quality, heavy-based non-stick pans, including a frying pan, a griddle pan or a wok with a close-fitting lid. Little, if any, oil is needed to stop food sticking to these pans as they cook. To reduce the oil in recipes even more than it already has been in this book, look out for the oil sprays sold with the cooking oils in many shops and supermarkets. Available in olive oil and sunflower oil versions, the oil sprays allow food to be almost dry-fried, with a negligible quantity of fat.

• Use lean cuts of meat such as beef and pork, trimming them of all obvious fat before adding them to a recipe. Trim the fat off bacon and cut the skin off chicken pieces.

• Several of the recipes in this book use cooked chicken: chicken breast in Spinach and Chicken Cannelloni (page 66) and Chicken and Orange Shells (page 70), for instance. A low-fat alternative to baking or grilling the chicken with oil or a knob of butter is to wrap it in foil, along with such flavourings as fresh herbs, a few spices and a sprinkling of wine, and bake it in a moderate oven. It can then be added to the chosen recipe. Another option is to poach the skinned chicken in chicken stock (see recipe on page 8) or simply in water, flavoured with plenty of fresh herbs.

• When a recipe calls for canned fish, such as the tuna in Pasta with Tuna and Tomato Sauce (page 65) or the sardines in Spaghetti with Sardines (page 62), choose varieties canned in brine, not oil. For recipes including anchovy fillets, such as Noodles with Fish Sauce (page 64), you can use anchovies preserved in salt, rather than the cans of anchovy fillets in oil, but wash off the salt before using.

• Shellfish is a good choice for seafood sauces to serve with pasta. Low in fat, it is also high in flavour. It is very important, particularly with bivalves like clams and mussels, that shellfish is cleaned and checked for freshness.

The following step-by-step picture sequence shows how to prepare the fresh mussels.

PREPARING MUSSELS

1 Wash the mussels thoroughly under cold running water then scrape away any barnacles with a sharp knife. Remove the beards and discard any mussels that are open and do not close when they are tapped with a knife or that have broken shells.

2 For 1 kg/2 lb mussels, put about 600 ml/1 pint water in a large saucepan and bring to the boil. Add the mussels, cover the pan and bring back to the boil.

3 Cook the mussels, shaking the pan occasionally, until the mussels open. Drain the mussels into a colander, reserving half of the cooking liquor. Transfer the mussels to a deep serving dish, discarding any that have not opened during cooking.

• Cook with polyunsaturated oils, such as olive, sunflower and vegetable oils which are used in the recipes in this book, rather than with cooking fats, lard or hard margarine. Avoid soft margarine and spreads containing hydrogenated vegetable oil, which has a high saturated fat content.

• Steam, grill, bake or microwave foods rather than fry them. Steaming or microwaving is particularly good for vegetables because there is no water in which vitamins can be lost.

• Use low-fat or fat-free stocks for soups and pasta sauces, avoiding stock cubes which tend to be salty and which contain fat. If you have no stock and need to use water instead, put additional flavour into the water with wine or cider, a few dashes of vinegar (balsamic vinegar is particularly good), tasty sauces such as soy, Teriyaki, Tabasco or Worcestershire, or plenty of fresh herbs.

THREE LOW-FAT STOCKS

These stocks are ideal for using in the recipes in this book.

CHICKEN STOCK

1 Put a 1.5 kg/3 lb chicken into a large saucepan with 2.4 litres/4 pints water and bring slowly to the boil. Remove any surface scum.

2 Add a bouquet garni, 1 small onion, peeled and stuck with 3 cloves, salt and pepper to taste and a small bunch of tarragon. Return to the boil, lower the heat and simmer gently for 1½ hours, covered, skimming regularly.

3 Strain the stock through fine muslin or a very fine strainer. Cool quickly and chill until required, removing any hardened fat from the surface of the stock before using it.

Note: Cut the skin off the cooled chicken and use the meat in salads or pasta dishes.

Makes 1 litre/1¾ pints.

VEGETABLE STOCK

1 Prepare and chop 3 medium potatoes, 1 medium onion, 2 leeks, 2 celery sticks and 2 medium carrots. Put them in a large saucepan with 1 small head of fennel, thinly sliced, fresh thyme and parsley and two bay leaves. Add 1.5 litres/2½ pints water. Bring slowly to the boil, then skim.

2 Add salt and pepper to taste. Simmer for about 1½ hours, covered, skimming the stock three or four times during cooking.

3 Strain the stock through fine muslin or a very fine strainer. Cool quickly and chill until needed.

Makes about 1 litre/1¾ pints.

FISH STOCK

1 Put 1 kg/2 lb fish trimmings (head, skin and bones) in a large saucepan with 1 small chopped onion, 2 chopped leeks, a bay leaf, parsley stalks, fennel sprigs and 2 or 3 strips of lemon rind. Add 1.2 litres/2 pints water. Bring to the boil and slowly skim off any surface scum.

2 Add 200 ml/⅓ pint dry white wine and salt and pepper to taste. Simmer very gently for 30 minutes, skimming the stock once or twice during cooking. Do not simmer for longer than 30 minutes, or the stock will be bitter.

3 Strain the stock through fine muslin or a very fine strainer. Cool quickly and keep chilled until needed.

Makes about 1 litres/1¾ pints.

LOW-FAT PASTA IN A LOW-FAT DIET

Most readers of this book will be using it because they want to reduce the fat in their diet. Not a lot will be achieved if the recipes here are simply added to an otherwise unchanged high-fat diet. Going low-fat requires one's diet to be rethought, with the overall fat content being reduced, rather than one kind of fat being replaced by another. Here are some tips on foods to avoid or replace and on foods lower in fat to use in their place.

DAIRY PRODUCTS

Whole milk, butter, cream, cheese and ice cream all contain significant amounts of saturated fats. Replacing them in the diet with foods containing polyunsaturated fats helps a little in the quest for healthy eating because the fats the latter contain are more healthy. Weight for weight, however, the polyunsaturated fats in margarine and safflower, sunflower and rapeseed oil have the same amount of fat and calories. Better to replace them, or at least reduce the amounts you use.

Replace whole milk with semi-skimmed or skimmed milk. Use fromage frais rather than cream when serving fresh fruits such as raspberries and strawberries for dessert. Substitute low-fat yogurt instead of cream in any sauces.

Leave cream and milk out of coffee and tea. Try a small strip of orange peel in black coffee, or a slice of lemon in tea.

Use low-fat or half-fat cheeses instead of full fat cheese. Unfortunately, there is no half-fat version of Parmesan, the perfect pasta cheese. Either use less of it, or try replacing it with a half-fat hard cheese, such as Cheddar.

If you enjoy ending a meal with a selection of cheese, choose reduced-fat Cheddar, Brie or mozzarella and serve cottage and curd cheeses for spreading. Serve on crispbread or rice cakes, without butter.

MEAT, MEAT PRODUCTS AND FISH

Use only the leanest cuts of meat such as beef, lamb and pork, trimming off all visible fat and skin. Don't forget venison, a low-fat red meat.

Read the labels carefully on all packets of sausages and processed meats, which can be very high in fat. Choose those with no more than 10 per cent fat by weight or 3 grams of fat per 25 g/1 oz.

Increase the amount of poultry, especially chicken and turkey on the menu, removing the skin before use. Eat a lot more fish, too, especially white fish like cod, haddock, plaice, halibut, sea bass and monkfish. Although oily fish such as salmon and mackerel contain more fats than white fish, the fats are polyunsaturated (called omega 3 type) and are thought to be beneficial in reducing levels of cholesterol in the blood.

FRUITS, VEGETABLES, GRAINS AND LEGUMES

These foods are generally low in fat, high in fibres and vitamins and without cholesterol and should all play major roles in low-fat cooking. Be careful that you do not detract from their value by serving high-fat foods with them.

Avoid using fat when cooking vegetables and do not add a knob of butter to cooked vegetables; instead, sprinkle them with fresh herbs or spices such as freshly ground black pepper.

Avoid using rich salad dressings with salads. Make your own dressings with low-fat yogurt or fromage frais, and use healthy oils such as olive oil.

Leave nuts and seeds out of salads accompanying pasta dishes. Unfortunately, Nature has not given us a low-fat nut, many of which are also high in calories. Although it is consoling to know that nuts and seeds do not contain cholesterol and their fats are usually unsaturated, it is best to avoid them in low-fat eating.

Soups and Starters

Italian Pasta and Bean Soup

175 g/6 oz smoked bacon, rinded and chopped
or lean salt pork, rinded and diced
1 onion, finely chopped
1 carrot, finely chopped
1 celery stick, finely chopped
125 g/4 oz pinto beans, soaked overnight
125 g/4 oz haricot beans, soaked overnight

2 garlic cloves, crushed
1.4 litres/2½ pints Vegetable Stock (see page 8)
1 small ham bone (knuckle)
250 g/8 oz dried tagliatelle, broken into
4–5 cm/1½–2 inch pieces
2 tablespoons finely chopped parsley
salt and pepper

1 Put the bacon or pork into a heavy saucepan and place it over a moderate heat until the fat runs. Increase the heat and continue cooking, stirring occasionally, until the bacon or pork is crisp. Remove with a slotted spoon and set aside.
2 Add the onion, carrot and celery to the pan. Cook for 10–15 minutes, stirring, until soft. Drain the beans and add to the pan with the garlic, bacon or pork and three-quarters of the stock. Bring to the boil, then add the bone, cover and simmer for 1½–2 hours until the beans are soft.
3 Remove the bone and cut the meat from it into cubes, discarding the skin and fat. Put the meat back into the soup and add the remaining stock. Bring back to the boil. Add the pasta and half the parsley and season to taste. Cook for 10–15 minutes, stirring occasionally, until the pasta is *al dente*. Serve sprinkled with the remaining parsley.

Serves 6
Preparation time: 30 minutes, plus soaking overnight
Cooking time: 2½–3 hours

kcal 327; kJ 1390; Protein 23 (g); Fat 4 (g); CHO 53 (g)

Bean and Mushroom Soup

- 125 g/4 oz haricot beans, soaked overnight and drained
- 125 g/4 oz red kidney beans, soaked overnight and drained
- 2 tablespoons oil
- 1 onion, sliced
- 1 garlic clove, crushed
- 125 g/4 oz button mushrooms, sliced
- 1.2 litres/2 pints Vegetable Stock (page 8)
- 175 g/6 oz broad beans, shelled
- 50 g/2 oz pasta, such as spirals or rings
- salt and pepper

1 Place the haricot and red kidney beans in separate saucepans, cover with cold water and bring to the boil. Simmer the haricot beans for 1½ hours and the kidney beans for 1 hour or until tender, adding salt towards the end of cooking.

2 Heat the oil in a large saucepan, add the onion and cook for about 5 minutes until soft. Add the garlic, mushrooms, Vegetable Stock, broad beans and season to taste with salt and pepper and simmer for 10 minutes. Stir in the pasta and the drained haricot beans and simmer for a further 15 minutes or until the pasta is *al dente*.

Serves 6
Preparation time: 2 hours, plus soaking overnight
Cooking time: about 30 minutes

kcal 227; kJ 962; Protein 15 (g); Fat 5 (g); CHO 33 (g)

Pasta and Lentil Soup

The lentils can be cooked and the sauce made the previous day, then the pasta added and cooked just before it is served.

- 250 g/8 oz small dried lentils, soaked overnight
- 175 g/6 oz canned tomatoes
- 2 garlic cloves, cut into 3–4 pieces
- small bunch of parsley, roughly chopped
- 250 g/8 oz pasta, such as tubetti or pasta mista
- salt

1 Drain the lentils and put them into a large saucepan, with enough water to come about 5 cm/2 inches over them. Add 1 teaspoon salt, bring to the boil and simmer until almost tender. The cooking time can vary, depending on the quality and type of lentils used.

2 Meanwhile, purée the tomatoes in a food processor. Heat a wok and dry fry the garlic for 3–6 minutes, stirring constantly. Transfer to a shallow baking dish and place in a preheated oven, 180°C (350°F), Gas Mark 4, for about 6 minutes until soft. Return to a saucepan and add the tomatoes, half of the parsley and salt to taste. Simmer gently for about 10 minutes.

3 When the lentils are ready, pour in the sauce, adding a little more water if necessary, enough to cover the pasta, then bring to the boil and add the pasta. Cook for 10–12 minutes until the pasta is *al dente*. Serve garnished with the remaining parsley.

Serves 4
Preparation time: 20 minutes, plus soaking overnight
Cooking time: about 1 hour
Oven temperature: 180°C (350°F), Gas Mark 4

kcal 387; kJ 1646; Protein 23 (g); Fat 2 (g); CHO 74 (g)

Consommé with Small Pasta

Make the consommé the day before, so that it can cool completely and all the fat can be removed.

- 2 carrots, sliced
- 1 celery stick, halved
- 1 potato, halved
- 1 ripe tomato, halved
- 1 onion, halved
- small bunch of parsley
- 500 g/1 lb chicken pieces, with skins removed
- 400 g/13 oz brisket of beef
- 1 teaspoon salt
- 375 g/12 oz anellini or capellini pasta

1 Put all the ingredients, except for the pasta and a sprig of parsley, into a large saucepan and add enough water to come three-quarters of the way up the sides of the pan. Bring to the boil and simmer very slowly for about 3 hours, topping up with more boiling water if the level falls below that of the meat.
2 Remove the chicken and beef from the pan and strain the consommé through a fine sieve into a bowl. Leave the soup to stand overnight and when it is completely cold skim the fat off the surface.
3 Return the strained consommé to a saucepan, bring to the boil and add the pasta. Cook for 10–12 minutes until the pasta is *al dente*. Garnish with the reserved parsley and serve.

Serves 6
Preparation time: 30 minutes, plus standing overnight
Cooking time: 3¼ hours

kcal 214; kJ 910; Protein 8 (g); Fat 1 (g); CHO 46 (g)

Pasta in Broth

- 250 g/8 oz chicken pieces, chopped, with skins removed
- 250 g/8 oz stewing beef, cubed
- 1.2 litres/2 pints water
- 1 carrot, roughly chopped
- 1 celery stick, chopped
- 1 large onion, studded with 4–6 cloves
- 1 garlic clove, halved
- 4–6 black peppercorns
- 1 bouquet garni
- 200 g/7 oz dried tiny soup pasta
- salt and pepper

TO GARNISH:
- celery leaves
- sprigs of marjoram

1 Put the chicken and beef in a large saucepan. Pour in the water and bring to the boil, skimming off any scum that rises to the surface.

2 Add the carrot, celery, onion, garlic, peppercorns and bouquet garni to the saucepan and season to taste. Bring back to the boil, then reduce the heat, half cover the saucepan and simmer very gently for 1–2 hours (the longer the stock is left to cook the more flavoursome the broth will be). Top up with more cold water from time to time if necessary.

3 Strain the stock through a fine sieve into a clean saucepan. Skim off any fat. Bring the stock to the boil and add the pasta. Cover the pan and boil for 10 minutes, or until the pasta is *al dente*. Taste and adjust the seasoning, if necessary. Serve the soup hot, garnished with celery leaves and marjoram sprigs.

Serves 4
Preparation time: 15 minutes
Cooking time: 1½–2½ hours

kcal 170; kJ 728; Protein 6 (g); Fat 1 (g); CHO 37 (g)

FREEZING IS RECOMMENDED
Freeze without the pasta in an airtight rigid container for up to 3 months. Defrost in a refrigerator overnight, then reheat until bubbling. Add the pasta and complete the recipe.

Vermicelli and Bean Soup

- 250 g/8 oz red kidney beans, soaked overnight and drained
- 1.8 litres/3 pints water
- 4 tablespoons tomato purée
- 2 tablespoons olive oil
- 1 onion, chopped
- 1 garlic clove, crushed
- 3 celery sticks, chopped
- 3 carrots, sliced
- 2 tomatoes, skinned and chopped
- 2 tablespoons chopped parsley
- 1 teaspoon dried oregano
- 125 g/4 oz vermicelli, broken into short lengths
- salt and pepper

1 Bring the beans, water and tomato purée to the boil in a large pan. Cover and simmer for 1½ hours. Heat a wok and dry fry the onion and garlic for 3–6 minutes. Transfer to a baking dish and soften in a preheated oven, 180°C (350°F), Gas Mark 4, for 6 minutes. Add to the beans with the vegetables and herbs. Season, cover and simmer for 20 minutes. Add the pasta and cook for 5 minutes until *al dente*.

Serves 6
Preparation time: 10 minutes, plus soaking overnight
Cooking time: about 2 hours
Oven temperature:180°C (350°F), Gas Mark 4

kcal 240; kJ 1010; Protein 12 (g); Fat 5 (g); CHO 39 (g)

Watercress and Vermicelli Soup

- 2 tablespoons vegetable oil
- 2 onions, sliced
- 2 bunches of watercress, roughly chopped
- 1.5 litres/2½ pints Chicken Stock (see page 8)
- 75 g/3 oz vermicelli, broken into short lengths
- 1 egg, hard-boiled and finely chopped
- salt and pepper

1 Heat the oil in a large saucepan, add the onion and watercress and cook gently for 5 minutes, then add the stock, salt and pepper and simmer for 20 minutes. Add the vermicelli and simmer for a further 5 minutes, or until it is *al dente*. Serve sprinkled with chopped hard-boiled egg.

Serves 6
Preparation time: 10 minutes
Cooking time: 30 minutes

kcal 104; kJ 432; Protein 3 (g); Fat 5 (g); CHO 12 (g)

Noodle Soup

- 1 litre/1¾ pints Chicken Stock (see page 8) or water
- 3 tablespoons medium dry sherry
- 1 tablespoon light soy sauce
- 1 garlic clove, crushed
- 2.5 cm/1 inch piece of fresh root ginger, peeled and chopped
- 80 g/2.8 oz packet dried instant noodles with wonton-flavoured soup base
- 200 g/7 oz spinach, stalks removed and torn into shreds
- 300 g/10 oz silken tofu, drained and cut into strips
- 2–3 teaspoons sesame seeds, according to taste
- salt and pepper

1 Pour the stock or water into a large saucepan. Add the packet of soup base from the instant noodles, sherry, soy sauce, garlic and ginger and bring to the boil.

2 Add the noodles and spinach and simmer for 3 minutes. Add the tofu and simmer for a further 1–2 minutes until it is heated through. Adjust the seasoning if necessary, and sprinkle with the sesame seeds before serving.

Serves 4
Preparation time: 10 minutes
Cooking time: about 10 minutes

kcal 167; kJ 700; Protein 11 (g); Fat 5 (g); CHO 18 (g)

Chinese Shredded Pork and Noodle Soup

The flavour of the Chicken Stock is important in this soup, so try to make your own if possible.

- 1.2 litres/2 pints Chicken Stock (see page 8)
- 2 tablespoons light soy sauce
- 1 tablespoon vinegar
- 1 tablespoon medium dry sherry
- 250 g/8 oz lean pork fillet, cut diagonally into 3.5 x 1 cm/1½ x ½ inch strips
- 3 spring onions, sliced diagonally
- 2.5 cm/1 inch piece of fresh root ginger, peeled and cut into very fine matchsticks
- 125 g/4 oz button mushrooms, thinly sliced
- 200 g/7 oz Chinese leaves, shredded
- 125 g/4 oz bean sprouts
- 125 g/4 oz medium egg noodles
- salt and pepper

1 Place the stock in a large saucepan and bring it to the boil. Add the soy sauce, vinegar, sherry, pork strips, spring onions, ginger and mushrooms. Stir once, cover the pan and simmer for 10 minutes, stirring occasionally.
2 Add the Chinese leaves and cook for 5 minutes. Add the bean sprouts and noodles and season with salt and pepper to taste. Cook for 5 minutes more, or until the noodles are tender. Taste and adjust the seasoning, if necessary. Serve with some extra soy sauce, if liked.

Serves 4
Preparation time: 15 minutes
Cooking time: 30 minutes

kcal 220; kJ 933; Protein 8 (g); Fat 5 (g); CHO 26 (g)

Prawn Ravioli in Fish Broth

Large fresh Mediterranean prawns are best for this oriental-inspired dish, which is a cross between a soup and a starter. Small frozen peeled prawns can be used, but you will need several in each ravioli. Make sure they are defrosted and thoroughly dried before use. Fish stock cubes can be used for the broth, but you will get a more authentic flavour if you make your own stock with some fish bones and heads and the shells from the prawns (see the recipe on page 9).

- 12 Mediterranean prawns, shelled and halved
- 2 tablespoons finely chopped fresh coriander
- 2 stalks lemon grass or finely pared rind of 2 limes or 1 large lemon
- 1 litre/1¾ pints Fish Stock (see page 9)
- salt and pepper

RAVIOLI DOUGH:
- 125 g/4 oz strong plain flour
- 2 pinches of salt
- 1 egg, beaten
- 1 tablespoon olive oil

TO GARNISH:
- sprigs of parsley
- pared lime rind (optional)

1 First make the ravioli dough. Sift the flour and salt into a bowl. Mix in the egg, then the oil. Turn the dough out on to a floured surface and knead with floured hands for about 10 minutes until it is shiny and smooth. Cut the dough in half and wrap one half in a damp tea towel. Roll the other half out to a paper-thin rectangle 36 x 24 cm/ 14½ x 9½ inches, reflouring the surface and the rolling pin as necessary. Cover with a damp tea towel.

2 Unwrap the second piece of dough and roll it out to a rectangle the same size as the first. Place the prawn halves on this piece of dough at regular intervals, four prawn halves across the width of the dough and six along the length. Sprinkle each prawn half with a little of the chopped coriander and salt and pepper to taste.

3 Brush the edges of the dough and all around each prawn half with water, then place the first piece of dough on top. Press it down firmly, especially around each prawn half, to make a good seal and exclude any air from the separate parcels of dough.

4 Cut around each prawn half with a serrated-edged ravioli wheel, either in round or square shapes. As each one is cut out, place it on a floured baking sheet, then leave to dry for 1–2 hours.

5 If using lemon grass, bruise it by pounding it with a pestle. Pour the Fish Stock into a large saucepan, bring it to the boil and add the lemon grass, if using, or the lime or lemon rind and the remaining coriander. Add the ravioli, stir well and bring back to the boil. Reduce the heat and boil for 5 minutes or until the pasta is *al dente*, stirring frequently so that the ravioli cook evenly. Taste the stock and adjust the seasoning, if necessary, before serving. Garnish with parsley and lime rind, if using.

Serves 4
Preparation time: 30 minutes, plus drying
Cooking time: 10 minutes

kcal 176; kJ 742; Protein 10 (g); Fat 5 (g); CHO 24 (g)

MICROWAVE
Prepare the ravioli dough as described then make the prawn-stuffed ravioli. Place the Fish Stock in a large bowl, cover and cook on High Power for 6–8 minutes or until boiling. Add the lemon grass, or the lime or lemon rind, and remaining coriander. Add the ravioli and cook for 4 minutes or until *al dente*. Leave to stand for 2 minutes. Taste and adjust the seasoning if necessary and serve.

Green Minestrone

- 125 g/4 oz haricot beans, soaked overnight and drained
- 2 tablespoons olive oil
- 2 leeks, sliced
- 1 garlic clove, crushed
- 2 tablespoons chopped parsley
- 2 tablespoons chopped mixed herbs
- 1.8 litres/3 pints water
- 2 celery sticks, chopped
- 4 tomatoes, skinned and chopped
- 2 potatoes, diced
- 50 g/2 oz ditali or other small pasta
- 125 g/4 oz fresh or frozen peas
- salt and pepper

1 Place the beans in a saucepan with enough water to cover. Bring to the boil, then cook for 1½ hours or until tender, adding salt towards the end of the cooking time.

2 Heat the oil in a saucepan, add the leeks, garlic and half of the parsley and mixed herbs and cook for 10 minutes. Add the water, celery, tomatoes, potatoes and season with salt and pepper. Simmer for 30 minutes. Add the pasta, peas and haricot beans and simmer for a further 15 minutes until the pasta is *al dente* and the vegetables tender. Stir in the remaining parsley and mixed herbs and serve at once.

Serves 6
Preparation time: 2 hours, plus soaking overnight
Cooking time: about 2½ hours

kcal 175; kJ 738; Protein 8 (g); Fat 5 (g); CHO 27 (g)

Minestrone

- 125 g/4 oz haricot beans, soaked overnight and drained
- 2 tablespoons olive oil
- 1 onion, chopped
- 250 g/8 oz courgettes, chopped
- 4 tomatoes, peeled and chopped
- 125 g/4 oz mushrooms, sliced
- 250 g/8 oz French beans, cut into 1 cm/½ inch lengths
- 125 g/4 oz cauliflower, divided into florets
- ½ small cabbage, shredded
- 1.8 litres/3 pints water
- 50 g/2 oz vermicelli, broken into short lengths
- 2 tablespoons pesto
- salt and pepper
- freshly grated Parmesan cheese, to garnish

1 Cook the beans in boiling water for 1½ hours or until tender, adding salt towards the end of the cooking time.
2 Heat the oil in a pan and fry the onion until soft. Add the remaining vegetables, measured water, and season with salt and pepper. Simmer for 30–40 minutes.
3 Add the pasta and haricot beans and cook for a further 4–5 minutes.
4 Stir in the pesto just before serving and garnish lightly with the Parmesan.

Serves 8
Preparation time: 10 minutes
Cooking time: about 2 hours, plus soaking overnight

kcal 144; kJ 600; Protein 7 (g); Fat 5 (g); CHO 18 (g)

Chinese-style Vermicelli

- 250 g/8 oz dried vermicelli
- 4 carrots, cut into fine matchsticks
- 4 courgettes, cut into fine matchsticks
- 125 g/4 oz small mangetout
- 5 teaspoons oil
- 4 spring onions, sliced diagonally
- 2.5 cm/1 inch piece of fresh root ginger, peeled and sliced into matchsticks
- 1–2 garlic cloves, crushed
- 4 tablespoons light soy sauce
- 1 tablespoon clear honey
- 1 tablespoon white wine vinegar
- 1 teaspoon coriander seeds, crushed
- salt and pepper
- parsley leaves, to garnish

1 Bring a large saucepan of salted water to the boil. Add the vermicelli, stir and bring back to the boil. Reduce the heat slightly and boil, uncovered, for 8–10 minutes, or until *al dente*, stirring occasionally.

2 Meanwhile, put the carrots, courgettes and mangetout into a colander or sieve and sprinkle with salt. Place the colander over the pan of boiling vermicelli. Cover the colander and steam the vegetables for about 5 minutes until they are tender but still crunchy. Remove the colander and set it aside. Drain the vermicelli when it is still *al dente*, and cut it into shorter lengths with kitchen scissors.

3 Heat the oil in a wok or deep frying pan. Add the spring onions and ginger and cook gently, stirring, until the ingredients give off a spicy aroma. Add the garlic, soy sauce, honey, wine vinegar and coriander seeds, stirring well. Add the vermicelli and vegetables. Increase the heat and vigorously toss the ingredients in the wok until they are evenly combined and very hot. Season with pepper to taste. Turn into a warm serving bowl and garnish with parsley leaves. Serve at once.

Serves 4
Preparation time: 15 minutes
Cooking time: 20 minutes

kcal 320; kJ 1336; Protein 9 (g); Fat 5 (g); CHO 61 (g)

Spaghetti with Anchovies

- 500 g/1 lb spaghetti
- 2 x 50 g/2 oz cans anchovies in oil, drained
- 1 garlic clove, crushed
- finely grated rind and juice of 1 orange
- pinch of sugar
- ½ tablespoon freshly grated Parmesan cheese
- 2 tablespoons chopped mint
- salt and pepper

1 Bring a large saucepan of salted water to the boil. Add the spaghetti, stir and cook for 10–12 minutes until *al dente*.

2 Meanwhile, chop the anchovies and add them to the pan with the garlic.

Stir with a wooden spoon, pressing the anchovies so that they break up and become almost puréed. Add the orange rind and juice, the sugar and pepper to taste. Stir the sauce vigorously until heated through and combined with the anchovies.

3 Drain the spaghetti well and turn it into a warm serving bowl. Pour over the sauce, add the Parmesan and half the mint and toss together quickly. Serve at once, sprinkled with the remaining mint.

Serves 6

Preparation time: 15 minutes
Cooking time: about 25 minutes

kcal 345; kJ 1463; Protein 15 (g); Fat 5 (g); CHO 64 (g)

MICROWAVE

Immerse the spaghetti in 1.2 litres/ 2 pints boiling salted water in a bowl and cook on High Power for 10–12 minutes, stirring once. Cover and leave to stand while preparing the anchovies. Place the anchovies in a bowl with the garlic and cook on High Power for 2 minutes, stirring once. Purée the mixture by beating with a spoon then add the orange rind and juice, sugar and pepper to taste. Drain the spaghetti and toss with the sauce, mint and Parmesan.

Spaghetti with Clam Sauce

- 1 x 400 g/13 oz can tomatoes
- 4 tablespoons dry red or white wine
- 2 tablespoons finely chopped parsley
- 2 teaspoons finely chopped basil
- 1 small onion, finely chopped
- 2 garlic cloves, crushed
- 250–300 g/8–10 oz spaghetti
- 1 x 300 g/10 oz can baby clams, well drained
- salt and pepper
- chopped parsley, to garnish

1 Place the canned tomatoes with their juice in a food processor or blender. Add the wine and herbs and work to a purée.

2 Heat a wok or heavy saucepan and dry fry the onion for 3–6 minutes, turning constantly. Add the garlic and puréed tomatoes. Season to taste. Cover and simmer gently for about 15 minutes, stirring occasionally.

3 Meanwhile, bring a large saucepan of salted water to the boil. Add the spaghetti, stir and cook for 10–12 minutes until *al dente*.

4 Stir the clams into the tomato sauce and heat them through. Adjust the seasoning if necessary. Drain the spaghetti well and turn it into a warmed serving bowl. Pour over the sauce and garnish with chopped parsley. Serve at once.

Serves 4
Preparation time: 15 minutes
Cooking time: about 30 minutes

kcal 370; kJ 1566; Protein 22 (g); Fat 2 (g); CHO 66 (g)

Paglia e Fieno with Tomato and Rosemary

Dried chillies taste very hot, so it is best to remove them before serving.

- 1 x 625 g/1¼ lb can of tomatoes
- 1 tablespoon olive oil
- 1 small carrot, finely chopped
- 1 small onion, finely chopped
- 1 celery stick, finely chopped
- about 4 tablespoons red wine
- 2 whole dried red chillies
- 250–300 g/8–10 oz fresh plain paglia e fieno pasta, coiled into nests
- 2 teaspoons chopped rosemary
- salt and pepper
- sprigs of rosemary, to garnish

1 Purée the tomatoes and their juice in a food processor or blender.
2 Heat the oil in a heavy saucepan. Add the carrot, onion and celery and cook gently, stirring frequently, for 15 minutes or until soft. Add the red wine, increase the heat and stir until the wine has been absorbed by the vegetables. Add the puréed tomatoes and the whole chillies, then season to taste and bring to the boil. Reduce the heat, cover, and simmer for 15–20 minutes until the sauce is quite thick.
3 Meanwhile, bring a large saucepan of salted water to the boil. Add the pasta, stir and cook for 3–4 minutes until *al dente*. Drain the pasta and turn it into a warm bowl. Remove the sauce from the heat and stir in the chopped

rosemary. Adjust the seasoning. Pour the sauce over the pasta and serve garnished with rosemary sprigs.

Serves 4

Preparation time: 15 minutes
Cooking time: about 50 minutes

kcal 277; kJ 1178; Protein 9 (g); Fat 4 (g); CHO 53 (g)

Tagliatelle Romana

- 1.5 litres/2½ pints Chicken Stock (see page 8)
- 250 g/8 oz tagliatelle
- 125 g/4 oz Quark cheese
- 1 garlic clove, crushed
- 50 g/2 oz smoked prosciutto, fat removed and cut into strips
- salt and pepper
- finely chopped parsley, to garnish

1 Put the Chicken Stock into a large saucepan and bring to the boil. Add the tagliatelle, stir and cook for 10–12 minutes until just *al dente*, then drain and turn into a hot serving dish.
2 Sieve the Quark and mix in the garlic and seasoning. Stir the cheese mixture into the tagliatelle, toss in the strips of prosciutto, garnish with parsley and serve immediately.

Serves 4
Preparation time: 30 minutes
Cooking time: 10–12 minutes

kcal 258; kJ 1096; Protein 16 (g); Fat 2 (g); CHO 48 (g)

Vegetarian
Pasta

Pasta with Spring Vegetables

200 g/7 oz broccoli florets, divided into
tiny sprigs

4 young carrots, thinly sliced

200 g/7 oz frozen petits pois

375 g/12 oz dried penne

200 g/7 oz small button mushrooms, quartered

6 tablespoons dry white wine

2 tablespoons finely chopped parsley

300 ml/½ pint very low-fat natural yogurt

1 tablespoon freshly grated Parmesan cheese

salt and pepper

1 Cook the broccoli and carrots in boiling salted water for 5–7 minutes until they are tender but still crunchy. Remove with a slotted spoon and drain. Add the petits pois to the water and bring back to the boil. Simmer for 3–4 minutes. Drain well.

2 Bring a large saucepan of salted water to the boil. Add the penne, stir and cook for 10–12 minutes until *al dente*.

3 Place the mushrooms, wine and parsley in a saucepan and season with salt and pepper. Cook for 8–10 minutes, stirring. Add the vegetables and toss over a high heat to heat through.

4 Drain the penne thoroughly and turn into a warm bowl. Add the low-fat yogurt and vegetables and toss quickly together. Divide the pasta equally among four warm soup bowls. Sprinkle the remaining Parmesan on top and serve at once.

Serves 4
Preparation time: 30 minutes
Cooking time: about 12 minutes

kcal 457; kJ 1940; Protein 24 (g); Fat 4 (g); CHO 83 (g)

Pasta Twists with Bean Sauce

Mixed bean salad is a combination of green, red kidney, black eye, borlotti and cannellini beans with chick peas, sweetcorn and red peppers.

- 1 small onion, finely chopped
- 1 x 185 g/6½ oz can pimentos (sweet red peppers), drained and thinly sliced
- 1 x 400 g/13 oz can chopped tomatoes with herbs
- 1 x 425 g/14 oz can mixed bean salad, drained
- 1 teaspoon tomato purée
- 375 g/12 oz dried wholewheat pasta twists or spirals
- 2 tablespoons chopped parsley
- salt and pepper
- sprigs of chervil, to garnish

1 Heat a wok or heavy frying pan and dry fry the onion for 3–6 minutes, stirring constantly.

2 Add the pimentos and stir-fry for 1–2 minutes. Add the tomatoes with their juice, the beans and tomato purée and season to taste. Stir well, and simmer, for about 15 minutes.

3 Meanwhile, bring a large saucepan of salted water to the boil. Add the pasta, stir and cook for 10–12 minutes until *al dente*.

4 Drain the pasta well and turn it into a warm bowl. Stir half of the parsley into the bean sauce. Taste and adjust the seasoning, if necessary, and pour the sauce over the pasta, tossing well. Divide the pasta and its sauce equally among four warm bowls. Scatter over the remaining parsley and serve at once, garnished with chervil sprigs.

Serves 4

Preparation time: 20 minutes
Cooking time: 10–12 minutes

kcal 460; kJ 1968; Protein 19 (g); Fat 4 (g); CHO 94 (g)

Tagliatelle Sicilienne

- 1 large aubergine, diced
- 1 tablespoon olive oil
- 2 onions, chopped
- 2 garlic cloves, chopped
- 1 x 400 g/13 oz can chopped plum tomatoes
- 2 teaspoons chopped basil
- 3.6 litres/6 pints water
- 375 g/12 oz fresh tagliatelle
- salt and pepper

1 Sprinkle the diced aubergine with salt and leave for 30 minutes to remove any bitter taste. Rinse in cold water and dry well with kitchen paper.
2 Heat the oil in a saucepan, add the onion, garlic and aubergines and cook for 2–3 minutes. Add the tomatoes and their juice, together with the basil, and season to taste. Simmer for 15–20 minutes.
3 Meanwhile, bring the water to the boil in a large pan and add salt to taste. Put in the pasta, stir, and cook for 3–4 minutes until just *al dente*.

4 Drain the pasta, turn it into a warm serving dish and top with the aubergine mixture.

Serves 4
Preparation time: 10 minutes, plus standing
Cooking time: 15–20 minutes

kcal 388; kJ 1650; Protein 14 (g); Fat 5 (g); CHO 77 (g)

Tomato Tagliatelle

- 500 g/1 lb fresh red tagliatelle
- 1 tablespoons vegetable oil
- 2 onions, sliced
- 2 garlic cloves, crushed
- 500 g/1 lb courgettes, thinly sliced
- 1 green pepper, cored, deseeded and sliced
- 2 large tomatoes, skinned and chopped
- 250 g/8 oz button mushrooms, sliced
- 2 tablespoons chopped parsley
- salt and pepper
- sprigs of oregano, to garnish

1 Bring a large saucepan of lightly salted water to the boil. Add the pasta, stir and cook for about 5 minutes, or until *al dente*. Drain the pasta, rinse with hot water to stop it becoming sticky, and drain again. Return the pasta to the pan and keep warm.
2 To make the sauce, heat the oil in a saucepan and cook the onions gently for 3 minutes, stirring once or twice. Add the garlic, courgettes and green pepper and cook for 3 minutes. Add the tomatoes and mushrooms, stir well, cover the pan and simmer for 10 minutes, or until the vegetables are just tender. Season with salt and pepper and stir in the parsley.
3 Turn the tagliatelle into a heated serving dish, pour on the sauce and toss well. Garnish with oregano sprigs and serve at once.

Serves 6
Preparation time: about 20 minutes
Cooking time: 25 minutes

kcal 342; kJ 1451; Protein 13 (g); Fat 4 (g); CHO 68 (g)

Spinach Noodles

- 250 g/8 oz low-fat pasta
- 1 onion, chopped
- 250 g/8 oz spinach, chopped
- 150 ml/¼ pint very low-fat natural yogurt
- 125 g/4 oz vegetarian Quark cheese
- 1 teaspoon lemon juice
- ¼ teaspoon grated nutmeg
- salt and pepper

1 Bring a large saucepan of salted water to the boil. Add the noodles, stir and cook for 10–12 minutes until *al dente*.

2 Meanwhile, dry fry the onion, turning constantly, until soft, but not browned. Add the spinach and cook for 2–3 minutes. Stir in the yogurt, Quark, lemon juice, nutmeg and salt and pepper, and cook over a low heat without boiling. Drain the noodles and add to the hot spinach sauce; toss well then serve immediately.

Serves 3
Preparation time: 10 minutes
Cooking time: 15 minutes

kcal 655; kJ 2785; Protein 48 (g); Fat 5 (g); CHO 133 (g)

Chicory, Orange and Pasta Salad

- 500 g/1 lb fresh tagliatelle, cut into short lengths
- 4 heads of chicory, sliced
- 6 large oranges, peeled and segmented
- 2 tablespoons chopped tarragon
- 4 tablespoons chopped chives

DRESSING:

- 3 teaspoons olive oil
- 2 tablespoons orange juice
- 2 tablespoons lemon juice
- ½ teaspoon coarse-grain mustard
- 1 teaspoon honey
- 1 teaspoon mixed herbs
- 1 teaspoon finely grated orange rind

1 Bring a large saucepan of salted water to the boil. Add the pasta, stir and cook for 4–5 minutes until *al dente*. Drain and cool quickly under cold running water. Drain thoroughly and place in a large bowl.
2 Mix together the dressing ingredients and pour over the pasta.
3 Stir in the chicory, orange segments and herbs. Transfer to a serving dish and serve immediately.

Serves 4
Preparation time: 15 minutes
Cooking time: about 5 minutes

kcal 540; kJ 2298; Protein 18 (g); Fat 5 (g); CHO 114 (g)

Pasta with Cauliflower

The breadcrumbs in this recipe are best when made from a 3–4 day old loaf of bread.

- 2 litres/3½ pints water
- 750 g/1½ lb cauliflower, divided into florets
- 425 g/14 oz mezze zite or macaroni
- 2 teaspoons olive oil
- 25 g/1 oz stale breadcrumbs
- salt and pepper

1 Bring the measured water and a little salt to the boil in a large saucepan, add the cauliflower and cook for 3 minutes. Add the pasta and cook for 10–12 minutes until *al dente*.
2 Drain the cauliflower and pasta and pile into a warm serving dish; keep hot. Heat the oil in a small saucepan, add the breadcrumbs and fry over a medium-high heat until well browned. Sprinkle over the cauliflower and pasta, season with pepper to taste and fold gently to mix. Serve immediately.

Serves 4
Preparation time: 10 minutes
Cooking time: about 15 minutes

kcal 463; kJ 1968; Protein 20 (g); Fat 5 (g); CHO 89 (g)

Pasta with Rich Tomato Sauce

- 1 large onion, sliced
- 1 garlic clove, crushed
- 750 g/1½ lb ripe tomatoes, skinned and chopped
- 1 tablespoon tomato purée
- 2 teaspoons caster or granulated sugar
- 2 tablespoons marjoram
- 150 ml/5 fl oz Vegetable Stock (see page 8)
- 250 g/8 oz lasagna verde
- salt and pepper

CRUNCHY DRESSING:
- 15 g/½ oz low-fat spread
- 1 tablespoon sunflower seeds
- 25 g/1 oz wholemeal breadcrumbs

1 Put the onion and garlic into a saucepan with a little water and cook for about 7 minutes until soft but not browned. Add the tomatoes, tomato purée, sugar, marjoram, stock, and season with salt and pepper. Half cover the pan and simmer gently for 25 minutes.

2 Remove the lid, increase the heat slightly and cook for 2–3 minutes to reduce the sauce – it should have a thick, rich consistency. Keep the sauce hot.

3 Meanwhile, bring a large saucepan of salted water to the boil, add the pasta, stir and cook for 10–12 minutes until *al dente*.

4 To make the crunchy dressing, heat the low-fat spread in a pan, add the sunflower seeds and brown them, then stir in the breadcrumbs. Shake the pan over the heat until the breadcrumbs are browned.

5 Drain the pasta thoroughly, turn into a warmed serving dish, spoon the hot sauce over and top with the crunchy dressing. Serve immediately,

Serves 4
Preparation time: 25 minutes
Cooking time: 30 minutes

kcal 286; kJ 1216; Protein 11 (g); Fat 5 (g); CHO 53 (g)

Penne with Aubergine

Be adventurous in selecting pasta shapes: rigatoni and mezze maniche (short sleeves) are other short and tubular types of pasta to choose from.

- 500 g/1 lb aubergine, cubed
- 250 g/8 oz penne
- 1 onion, chopped
- 2 garlic cloves, crushed
- 1 teaspoon mustard powder
- 1 tablespoon tomato purée
- 1 x 400 g/13 oz can tomatoes
- ½ teaspoon oregano
- 1 tablespoon chopped parsley
- salt and pepper

1 Put the aubergine in a colander and sprinkle with salt. Leave for 30 minutes to remove any bitter taste, rinse and pat dry with kitchen paper.
2 Bring a large saucepan of salted water to the boil. Add the pasta, stir and cook for 10–12 minutes until *al dente*. Drain and keep warm.
3 Meanwhile, simmer the onion and garlic in a little water for 3–6 minutes, stirring constantly. Transfer into a shallow baking dish and place in a preheated oven, 180°C (350°F), Gas Mark 4, for about 6 minutes until soft. Return to a saucepan.
4 Add the aubergine to the saucepan and cook, stirring, until lightly browned. Stir in the mustard, tomato purée, tomatoes and their juice, herbs and pepper to taste. Simmer gently for 10 minutes until the aubergine is cooked, stirring occasionally. Pour the sauce over the pasta and serve at once.

Serves 4
Preparation time: 5 minutes, plus standing

Cooking time: 30–35 minutes
Oven temperature: 180°C (350°F), Gas Mark 4

kcal 260; kJ 1110; Protein 10 (g); Fat 2 (g); CHO 54 (g)

Pasta Syracuse Style

- 1 large onion, sliced
- 2 garlic cloves, crushed
- 500 g/1 lb courgettes, chopped
- 1 green pepper, cored, deseeded and chopped
- 1 x 400 g/13 oz can tomatoes, drained and roughly chopped
- 125 g/4 oz black olives, pitted
- 3 anchovy fillets, finely chopped*
- 1 tablespoon chopped parsley
- 2 teaspoons chopped marjoram
- salt and pepper
- 500 g/1 lb low-fat pasta
- few sprigs of flat leaf parsley, to garnish

1 Heat a large frying pan or wok and dry fry the onion and garlic for 3–6 minutes, turning constantly, until soft. Add the courgettes and cook for 10 minutes. Add the green pepper, tomatoes, olives, anchovies, parsley, marjoram and salt and pepper to taste. Bring to the boil, stirring. Cover the pan and simmer while cooking the pasta.
2 Meanwhile, bring a large saucepan of salted water to the boil. Add the pasta, stir and cook for 10–12 minutes until *al dente*. Drain well and place in a warm serving dish. Add the sauce and toss lightly together. Garnish with the parsley and serve at once.

Serves 6
Preparation time: 15 minutes
Cooking time: about 30 minutes

kcal 345; kJ 1464; Protein 13 (g); Fat 4 (g); CHO 69 (g)
*contains fish, unsuitable for vegans

Pasta Bows with Tomatoes and Mushrooms

This simple dish is ideal for children, who will enjoy it even more if it is made with tri-coloured pasta – plain, spinach and tomato-flavoured.

- 175 g/6 oz pasta bows
- salt and pepper

SAUCE:

- 1 teaspoon sunflower oil
- 1 small onion, finely chopped
- 125 g/4 oz mushrooms, sliced
- 1 x 400 g/13 oz can tomatoes
- 1 tablespoon chopped basil (optional)
- salt and pepper

1 Bring a large saucepan of salted water to the boil. Add the pasta, stir and cook for 10–12 minutes until *al dente*. Drain and keep warm.
2 Meanwhile, make the sauce. Heat the oil in a saucepan, add the sliced onion and mushrooms and sauté for 5 minutes. Stir in the tomatoes and cook gently, uncovered, for 15 minutes to reduce the sauce. Add the basil, if using, and simmer for a further 5 minutes. Season to taste, pour over the pasta bows and serve.

Serves 2
Preparation time: 10 minutes
Cooking time: 25 minutes

kcal 364; kJ 1548; Protein 14 (g); Fat 4 (g); CHO 74 (g)

Pasta with Ratatouille Sauce

This sauce can be served cold as a starter, without the pasta.

- 1 large onion, chopped
- 1 garlic clove, crushed
- 500 g/1 lb courgettes, sliced
- 1 large aubergine, diced
- 1 green pepper, cored, deseeded and diced
- 500 g/1 lb tomatoes, skinned and chopped
- 1 tablespoon chopped oregano or basil
- 500 g/1 lb low-fat spaghetti
- 1 tablespoon chopped parsley, to garnish
- salt and pepper

1 Put all the ingredients, except the pasta and parsley, into a large saucepan. Add enough water to cover the vegetables and cook gently, stirring occasionally, for 30 minutes until the vegetables are tender and the juices have thickened slightly.
2 Meanwhile, bring a large saucepan of salted water to the boil. Add the pasta, stir and cook for 10–12 minutes until just *al dente*. Drain and place in a warmed serving dish.
3 Taste the sauce and adjust the seasoning if necessary, then pour over the pasta. Garnish with the parsley and serve hot.

Serves 4
Preparation time: 15–20 minutes
Cooking time: 35 minutes

kcal 509; kJ 2168; Protein 19 (g); Fat 4 (g); CHO 107 (g)

Bean and Pasta Curry

Curry sauce improves with keeping and can be made the day before, and then simply reheated while the pasta cooks. Either way, a substantial meal can be made in about 30 minutes. Serve the curry with some side dishes such as banana slices that have been sprinkled with lemon juice, cucumber slices and mango chutney. The sauce can be reheated and served with rice.

- 150 g/5 oz pasta quills or twists
- 2 x 400 g/13 oz cans red kidney beans
- salt

SAUCE:
- 1 tablespoon vegetable oil
- 3 onions, chopped
- 2 garlic cloves, crushed
- 3 tablespoons curry powder
- ½ teaspoon ground cumin
- ½ teaspoon ground coriander
- ½ teaspoon chilli powder
- 2 teaspoons grated fresh root ginger (optional)
- 2 tablespoons wholemeal flour
- 900 ml/1½ pints Vegetable Stock (see page 8)
- 1 tablespoon lemon juice

1 To make the sauce, heat the oil in a saucepan with a lid and gently fry the onion and garlic for 2–3 minutes. Stir in the curry powder, cumin, coriander, chilli powder, ginger and flour and cook for 1 minute. Pour in the Vegetable Stock and lemon juice, bring to the boil, then cover and simmer gently for 25 minutes. Taste and add salt if necessary.

2 Meanwhile, bring a large saucepan of salted water to the boil. Add the pasta, stir and cook for 10–12 minutes until *al dente*. Drain and rinse. Drain the kidney beans, reserving the liquid for thinning the sauce.

3 Add the pasta and beans to the sauce, stirring them in gently. If the sauce is too thick, thin with the reserved bean liquid.

Serves 4
Preparation time: 20 minutes
Cooking time: 30 minutes

kcal 305; kJ 1293; Protein 13 (g); Fat 5 (g); CHO 56 (g)

Pasta with Broad Beans and Greens

- 250 g/8 oz shelled young broad beans
- 1 tablespoons olive oil
- 1 red onion, finely chopped
- 3 garlic cloves, finely chopped
- 3 sage leaves, finely chopped
- ½ teaspoon dried chilli flakes
- 875 g/1¾ lb spring greens, kale or Swiss chard, stalks removed and leaves finely shredded
- 500 g/1 lb conchiglie, penne or gnocchi
- salt and pepper

1 Plunge the broad beans into boiling water for 2 minutes. Drain under cold running water, then slip off the outer skins if they are tough.

2 Heat the oil in a large frying pan, add the onion and fry gently until just soft. Add the garlic, sage and chilli flakes.

3 Add the greens to the pan and toss the leaves until they are coated with oil. Cover and cook over a moderate heat for 7–10 minutes, until the greens are just tender, adding a little water if the mixture becomes too dry. Stir in the beans and season to taste with salt and pepper.

4 Bring a large saucepan of salted water to the boil. Add the pasta, stir and cook for 10–12 minutes until *al dente*. Drain and toss with the green vegetables. Serve at once.

Serves 6
Preparation time: 10 minutes
Cooking time: about 25 minutes

kcal 387; kJ 1638; Protein 18 (g); Fat 5 (g); CHO 72 (g)

Pasta with Uncooked Tomato Sauce and Basil

- 500 g/1 lb ripe plum tomatoes, skinned
- 4 teaspoons olive oil
- 1 garlic clove, crushed
- bunch of basil
- 375 g/12 oz penne, conchiglie or farfalle
- salt

1 Put the tomatoes into a food processor or blender and purée briefly. Add the oil and crushed garlic.

2 Wash and dry the basil leaves, discarding the stalks. Tear the leaves into small pieces, and add to the sauce. Leave the sauce to stand for about 30 minutes, then add salt to taste and stir well.

3 Bring a large saucepan of salted water to the boil. Add the pasta, stir and cook for 10–12 minutes until *al dente*. Drain and transfer to a warm serving dish. Pour the sauce over the top and serve immediately.

Serves 4
Preparation time: 10 minutes, plus standing
Cooking time: about 12 minutes

kcal 347; kJ 1476; Protein 11 (g); Fat 5 (g); CHO 68 (g)

Spaghetti Peperonata

This delicious spaghetti has a fresh, spicy flavour and is perfect for a winter's lunch or supper.

- 300–375 g/10–12 oz spaghetti

SAUCE:

- 2 tablespoons olive oil
- 3 onions, finely chopped
- 2 garlic cloves, finely chopped
- 1 x 400 g/13 oz can chopped plum tomatoes
- 1 tablespoon tomato purée
- 1 tablespoon chopped oregano
- 2 bay leaves
- 1 green pepper, cored, deseeded and diced
- 1 red pepper, cored, deseeded and diced
- salt and pepper

1 First make the sauce: heat the oil in a saucepan and add the onion and garlic and cook for 5 minutes.
2 Add the tomatoes with their juice, the tomato purée, oregano, bay leaves and salt and pepper to taste. Simmer for 10 minutes, then add the diced red and green peppers. Cook for 10 minutes, or until the peppers are just soft. Remove the bay leaves before serving.
3 Meanwhile, bring a large saucepan of salted water to the boil. Add the spaghetti, stir and cook for 10–12 minutes until *al dente*.
4 Drain the pasta thoroughly, rinse with hot water and drain again. Pile on to a heated dish or individual plates. Top with the sauce and serve with a bowl of freshly grated Parmesan or other cheese.

Serves 4
Preparation time: 15 minutes
Cooking time: 35 minutes

kcal 370; kJ 1575; Protein 14 (g); Fat 2 (g); CHO 79 (g)

Bucatini del Buongustaio

Bucatini is a long pasta, not unlike spaghetti, which could be substituted if you prefer.

- 250–375 g/8–12 oz bucatini

SAUCE:

- 1 tablespoons olive oil
- 1 large onion, finely chopped
- 2 garlic cloves, finely chopped
- 1 aubergine, peeled and diced
- 125 g/4 oz mushrooms, sliced
- 1 x 400 g/13oz can chopped plum tomatoes
- sprig of sage
- salt and pepper

1 To make the sauce, heat the oil in a saucepan, add the onion, garlic and aubergine and cook for 5 minutes, then add the mushrooms and tomatoes, plus the juice from the can. Add the sage and a little salt and pepper. Cover the pan and cook gently for 15 minutes. Remove the sage.

2 Meanwhile, bring a large saucepan of salted water to the boil. Add the pasta, stir and cook for 10–12 minutes until *al dente*. Drain the pasta and add to the sauce.

3 Heat the pasta with the sauce for 1 minute, stirring gently to blend the two together, then serve at once.

Serves 4
Preparation time: 20 minutes
Cooking time: about 12 minutes

kcal 390; kJ 1663; Protein 14 (g); Fat 5 (g); CHO 77 (g)

Spaghetti with Garlic and Chilli

- 2 tablespoons olive oil
- 4 garlic cloves, finely chopped
- 1 red chilli, deseeded and chopped
- 500 g/1 lb spaghetti
- 2 tablespoons chopped parsley
- pepper

1 Heat the oil in a saucepan, add the garlic and chilli and fry gently for 1–2 minutes.

2 Bring a large saucepan of salted water to the boil. Add the pasta, stir and cook until *al dente*, 10–12 minutes. Drain and toss with the garlic mixture and the parsley. Season with black pepper and serve immediately.

Serves 6
Preparation time: 10 minutes
Cooking time: about 12 minutes

kcal 320; kJ 1354; Protein 10 (g); Fat 5 (g); CHO 62 (g)

Spaghetti with Mushrooms and Herbs

This is a simple, easy-to-cook lunch or supper dish.

- 2 teaspoons olive oil
- 75 g/3 oz onion, finely sliced
- 1 garlic clove, crushed
- 175 g/6 oz mushrooms, finely sliced
- 1 tablespoon mixed herbs
- 1 teaspoon dried sage, oregano or thyme
- 2 tablespoons white wine
- 200 g/7 oz spaghetti
- salt and pepper

1 Heat the oil in a saucepan, add the onion and garlic and fry gently for 2–3 minutes.
2 Add the mushrooms, then the herbs and season with salt and pepper. Continue to fry gently for a few minutes until the mushrooms have softened and darkened, add the white wine and simmer for about 5 minutes.
3 Meanwhile, bring a large saucepan of salted water to the boil. Add the pasta, stir and cook for 10–12 minutes until *al dente*.
4 Drain the pasta and pile into a warmed serving dish. Toss with the sauce and serve immediately.

Serves 2
Preparation time: 8–10 minutes
Cooking time: 10–12 minutes

kcal 404; kJ 1715; Protein 14 (g); Fat 5 (g); CHO 78 (g)

Spaghetti with Lentil Bolognese Sauce

Unlike some types of lentils, green lentils do not need lengthy pre-soaking. Simply rinse, then cook.

- 375 g/12 oz spaghetti
- 15 g/½ oz low-fat spread

SAUCE:
- 250 g/8 oz whole green lentils
- 2 teaspoons vegetable oil
- 2 onions, chopped
- 2 garlic cloves, crushed
- 2 celery sticks, chopped
- 2 carrots, finely diced
- 2 tablespoons tomato purée
- salt and pepper

1 To make the sauce, rinse the lentils, place in a pan, cover with water and bring to the boil. Simmer gently for about 40 minutes until tender. Drain, reserving the liquid.
2 Heat the oil in a large saucepan, add the onions and cook for 5 minutes, until soft then add the garlic, celery and carrots. Cook the vegetables, covered, for 15 minutes, until tender.
3 Stir in the lentils, tomato purée, salt and pepper and a little of the reserved lentil cooking liquid to make a thick, soft consistency. Simmer the sauce for about 10 minutes, adding more liquid if necessary.
4 Bring a large saucepan of salted water to the boil. Add the spaghetti, stir and cook for 10–12 minutes until

al dente. Drain the spaghetti, then return to the saucepan with the low-fat spread and season with pepper. Make sure the spaghetti is hot, then turn it on to a hot serving plate and pour the sauce on top.

Serves 4
Preparation time: 60 minutes
Cooking time: 45 minutes

kcal 439; kJ 1864; Protein 18 (g); Fat 5 (g); CHO 85 (g)

Pasta al Pomodoro

- 1 tablespoon olive oil
- 2 celery stalks, finely chopped
- 1 large carrot, finely chopped
- 1 small onion, finely chopped
- 2 garlic cloves, crushed
- 1 kg/2 lb ripe plum tomatoes, roughly chopped
- 1 teaspoon caster sugar
- 2 tablespoons chopped basil
- 500 g/1 lb spaghetti or linguine
- salt and pepper
- torn basil leaves, to garnish
- freshly grated Parmesan cheese, to serve

1 Heat the oil in a saucepan, add the celery, carrot, onion and garlic and fry gently for 5 minutes until softened.
2 Stir in the tomatoes, sugar and basil, and season to taste with salt and pepper. Bring to the boil, cover and simmer gently for 30 minutes.
3 Transfer the sauce to a food processor or blender and purée. Rub the purée through a sieve.
4 Bring a large saucepan of salted water to the boil. Add the pasta, stir and cook for 10–12 minutes until *al dente*. Drain and toss with the sauce. Transfer to a serving dish, garnish with torn basil leaves and serve immediately with a little Parmesan.

Serves 6
Preparation time: 15 minutes
Cooking time: 45 minutes

kcal 344; kJ 1463; Protein 12 (g); Fat 4 (g); CHO 69 (g)

Broccoli Sauce with Chilli

- 500 g/1 lb broccoli florets
- 500g/1 lb fusilli, orechiette or conchiglie
- dried chilli flakes, to taste
- 25 g/1 oz low-fat spread
- salt and pepper

1 Put the broccoli florets into a large pan of lightly salted boiling water and cook for 3 minutes until just tender. Drain and break into smaller pieces. Dice the stalks.
2 Bring a large saucepan of salted water to the boil. Add the pasta, stir and cook for 10–12 minutes until *al dente*. Drain and transfer to a warm serving dish, reserving a little of the pasta water.
3 Add the broccoli, chilli flakes and low-fat spread. Season to taste with salt and pepper. Toss well before serving, adding a little pasta water, if necessary, to keep the mixture moist.

Serves 6
Preparation time: 10 minutes
Cooking time: about 15 minutes

kcal 329; kJ 1395; Protein 14 (g); Fat 4 (g); CHO 63 (g)

Corsican Cannelloni

- 750 ml/1¼ pints boiling water
- ½ teaspoon vegetable oil
- 8 sheets no-need-to-precook lasagne verde
- 1 x 425 g/14 oz can ratatouille
- 125 g/4 oz frozen broad beans
- 2 teaspoons chopped fresh mixed herbs
- 1 x 400 g/13 oz can chopped tomatoes
- pepper
- 50 g/2 oz low-fat Cheddar cheese, grated, to serve

1 Pour the boiling water into a large, shallow, ovenproof dish and add the oil. Slide the sheets of lasagne into the dish and leave them for a few minutes to soften.

2 Put the ratatouille and beans into a saucepan of boiling water and cook for about 10 minutes, or until done. Drain well. Add the herbs and pepper to taste.

3 Remove the lasagne sheets and drain, then spread them on a clean work surface. Divide the vegetable filling among the lasagne sheets, then roll them up to make cannelloni.

4 Place the cannelloni in a shallow ovenproof dish and spoon over the chopped tomatoes. Cook in a preheated oven, 180°C (350°F), Gas Mark 4, for 30 minutes.

5 To serve, sprinkle the cannelloni with the grated cheese and place under a preheated grill until browned.

Serves 4

Preparation time: 15 minutes
Cooking time: 50 minutes
Oven temperature: 180°C (350°F), Gas Mark 4

kcal 435; kJ 1848; Protein 20 (g); Fat 5 (g); CHO 83 (g)

FREEZER TIP

Cover the cannelloni with foil and freeze for up to 3 months. Reheat from frozen in a moderate oven, 180°C (350°F), Gas Mark 4, for about 30 minutes, then top with the cheese and place under a hot grill to brown.

Rigatoni with Courgette Sauce

If any courgette flowers are available, they can be washed, sliced and added to the courgettes and onions while frying. The flowers have a very delicate flavour.

- 2 teaspoons olive oil
- 2 onions, finely chopped
- 8 courgettes, thinly sliced
- 500 g/1 lb rigatoni
- 1 tablespoon freshly grated Parmesan cheese
- salt

1 First make the sauce. Heat the oil in a large frying pan, add the onions and fry gently for about 5 minutes until soft and transparent. Add the courgettes after 3 minutes and fry them gently until just tender, stirring frequently to prevent them sticking. Cover the pan if the courgettes start to burn on the outside before being cooked through. Add salt to taste.

2 Meanwhile, bring a large saucepan of salted water to the boil. Add the rigatoni, stir and cook for 10–12 minutes until *al dente*. Drain the pasta, reserving a small quantity of the cooking water. Transfer the rigatoni to a warmed serving dish and mix in the courgettes and onions, adding a ladleful of the cooking water and the Parmesan to form a moist, creamy mixture. Serve immediately with a little extra Parmesan, if liked.

Serves 4
Preparation time: 15 minutes
Cooking time: 15–20 minutes

kcal 414; kJ 1758; Protein 16 (g); Fat 5 (g); CHO 82 (g)

Fish and Seafood Pasta

Pasta Twists with Mussels

1 kg/2 lb mussels

300 ml/½ pint water

150 ml/¼ pint dry white wine

1 bouquet garni

375 g/12 oz wholewheat twists, or other
pasta shapes

300 ml/½ pint natural yogurt

2 tablespoons chopped parsley

salt and pepper

lemon balm, to garnish

1 Thoroughly scrub the mussels in several bowls of clean water and pull off the beards. Tap the mussels and discard any that do not close. Put them into a large saucepan with the water and wine, bring to the boil, cover the pan and steam for 5–6 minutes, or until the shells have opened. Drain the mussels and reserve the cooking liquid. Discard any unopened mussels.

2 Pour the mussel liquid into a saucepan, add the bouquet garni, bring to the boil and fast-boil for 10 minutes, or until reduced by two-thirds. Discard the bouquet garni.

3 Remove the mussels from their shells, leaving about 8 in the shell to use as a garnish.

4 Bring a large saucepan of salted water to the boil. Add the pasta, stir and cook for 10–12 minutes until *al dente*. Drain, refresh in hot water, then drain again.

5 Put the pasta and mussels into a saucepan and season with pepper. Toss well. Beat the reserved mussel liquid with the yogurt, stir in the parsley and pour over the pasta. Toss well. Turn the pasta into a heated serving dish and garnish with lemon balm and the reserved mussels.

Serves 4

Preparation time: 1 hour

Cooking time: 30 minutes

kcal 428; kJ 1820; Protein 28 (g); Fat 4 (g); CHO 75 (g)

Pasta with Sea Bass

- 1 teaspoon olive oil
- 1 garlic clove, finely chopped
- 60 g/2½ oz green pepper, cored, deseeded and chopped
- 60 g/2½ oz onion, finely chopped
- 1 x 250 g/8 oz can tomatoes
- 1 tablespoon lemon juice
- 1 tablespoon chopped basil
- 4 sea bass fillets, weighing 125 g/4 oz each
- 300 g/10 oz penne
- salt and pepper

1 Heat the oil in a frying pan and add the garlic, green pepper and onion. Stir constantly for about 5 minutes until softened. Add the tomatoes and their juice, lemon juice and basil and cook for a further 5 minutes, breaking up the tomatoes with a wooden spoon,
2 Arrange the fillets in a single layer in a shallow baking dish and pour over the sauce. Cover the dish with foil and place in a preheated oven, 180°C (350°F), Gas Mark 4, and bake for about 15–20 minutes, or until the fish flakes easily.
3 Meanwhile, bring a large saucepan of lightly salted water to the boil. Add the pasta, stir and cook for 10–12 minutes until *al dente*.

4 Drain the pasta and turn into a warm serving dish. Add the flaked fish and its sauce, toss gently and serve at once.

Serves 4
Preparation time: 30 minutes
Cooking time: about 45 minutes
Oven temperature:180°C (350°F), Gas Mark 4

kcal 406; kJ 1720; Protein 34 (g); Fat 5 (g); CHO 59 (g)

Fettucine with Prawn Sauce

- 1 onion, chopped
- 2 garlic cloves, crushed
- 500 g/1 lb tomatoes, skinned and chopped
- ½ teaspoon dried basil
- 375 g/12 oz peeled prawns
- 150 ml/¼ pint white wine
- 2 tablespoons chopped parsley
- 500 g/1 lb fettucine
- salt and pepper

1 Put the onion and garlic into a saucepan with a little water and simmer until soft.

2 Add the tomatoes and basil, season with salt and pepper and simmer gently for 5 minutes. Stir in the prawns, wine and parsley and simmer for a further 10 minutes.

3 Bring a large saucepan of salted water to the boil. Add the pasta, stir and cook for 10–12 minutes until *al dente*.

4 Drain the pasta and place on a warm serving dish. Pour over the prawn sauce and serve at once.

Serves 4

Preparation time: 15 minutes
Cooking time: about 20 minutes

kcal 579; kJ 2460; Protein 37 (g); Fat 4 (g); CHO 98 (g)

Spaghetti with Sardines

- 1 onion, chopped
- 500 g/1 lb tomatoes, skinned and chopped
- 1 garlic clove, crushed
- ½ teaspoon saffron, soaked in 4 tablespoons boiling water
- 1 x 150 g/5 oz can sardines in brine
- 500 g/1 lb spaghetti
- salt and pepper

1 Heat a griddle pan or wok and dry fry the onion, turning constantly for 3–6 minutes, until soft. Add the tomatoes, garlic, the saffron with its water, sardines and salt and pepper to taste and simmer gently for 20 minutes.
2 Bring a large saucepan of salted water to the boil. Add the pasta, stir and cook for 10–12 minutes until *al dente*. Drain and mix with the sardine sauce. Serve immediately.

Serves 6
Preparation time: 20 minutes
Cooking time: about 40 minutes

kcal 346; kJ 1469; Protein 16 (g); Fat 4 (g); CHO 69 (g)

Pasta with Mediterranean Fish Sauce

- 1 small onion, finely chopped
- 2 garlic cloves, finely chopped
- 1 small red pepper, cored, deseeded and diced
- 1 small green pepper, cored, deseeded and diced
- 1 x 400 g/13 oz can chopped tomatoes
- 4 tablespoons finely chopped flat-leaf parsley
- 500 g/1 lb cod, cubed
- 500 g/1 lb rigatoni or penne
- salt and pepper

1 Heat a wok and dry fry the onion, garlic and pepper for 3–6 minutes, turning constantly, until soft.
2 Stir in the tomatoes, parsley and fish, and season to taste. Simmer, uncovered, until the fish is just tender.
3 Bring a large saucepan of salted water to the boil. Add the pasta, stir and cook for 10–12 minutes until *al dente*. Drain and toss with half of the sauce. Transfer to a warm serving dish. Spoon the remaining sauce over the top and serve immediately.

Serves 6
Preparation time: 10 minutes
Cooking time: 25–30 minutes

kcal 372; kJ 1640; Protein 26 (g); Fat 2 (g); CHO 66 (g)

Noodles with Fish Sauce

- 10 canned anchovy fillets
- 2–3 tablespoons skimmed milk
- 25 g/1 oz low-fat spread
- 1 large onion, chopped
- 2 garlic cloves, thinly sliced
- 150 ml/¼ pint dry white wine
- 250 ml/8 fl oz Fish Stock (see page 9)
- 175 g/6 oz cooked peeled prawns
- 2–3 tablespoons chopped parsley
- 500 g/1 lb fresh low-fat noodles
- salt and pepper

TO GARNISH:

- anchovy fillets
- whole prawns

1 Wash the anchovies in water and dry with kitchen paper. Put them into a bowl with the milk and leave to soak for 30 minutes. Drain the anchovies, chop and set aside.

2 Melt half of the low-fat spread in a saucepan, add the onion and cook for about 10 minutes, stirring, until golden brown. Add the garlic and cook for 1 minute. Add the wine, bring to the boil and cook rapidly until reduced by half. Add the Fish Stock, anchovies, prawns, and salt and pepper to taste and cook, uncovered, for 2 minutes. Remove the pan from the heat and stir in the parsley.

3 Bring a large saucepan of salted water to the boil. Add the noodles, stir and cook for 4–5 minutes until *al dente*. Drain thoroughly and turn into a warm serving dish. Add the remaining low-fat spread and toss well.

4 Reheat the sauce for 1 minute, then pour over the noodles and toss well. Garnish with anchovy fillets and whole prawns.

Serves 6

Preparation time: 15 minutes, plus soaking
Cooking time: 30 minutes

kcal 370; kJ 1572; Protein 19 (g); Fat 5 (g); CHO 64 (g)

Pasta with Tuna and Tomato Sauce

- 1 garlic clove, chopped
- 1 x 200 g/7 oz can tuna in brine, drained and coarsely flaked
- 3 tablespoons chopped parsley
- 2 tablespoons tomato purée
- 250 ml/8 fl oz Fish Stock (see page 9)
- 500g/1 lb rigatoni, penne or macaroni
- salt and pepper

1 Heat a large frying pan or wok and dry fry the garlic for 3–6 minutes, turning constantly, until soft and just beginning to colour. Add the flaked tuna, 2 tablespoons of the parsley, the tomato purée and Fish Stock. Season to taste with salt and pepper. Simmer gently for 15 minutes.

2 Meanwhile, bring a large saucepan of salted water to the boil. Add the pasta, stir and cook for 10–12 minutes until *al dente*. Drain, mix with the tuna sauce and transfer to a serving dish.

3 Sprinkle with the remaining chopped parsley and serve at once.

Serves 4
Preparation time: 10 minutes
Cooking time: 30–35 minutes

kcal 482; kJ 1369; Protein 27 (g); Fat 3 (g); CHO 94 (g)

Meat Pasta

Spinach and Chicken Cannelloni

12 dried cannelloni tubes

25 g/1 oz half-fat Cheddar cheese, grated

FILLING:

250 g/8 oz fresh leaf spinach, washed

2 onions, finely chopped

150 g/5 oz cooked chicken breast, minced

125 g/4 oz low-fat cottage cheese

1 teaspoon ground cinnamon

salt and pepper

TOMATO SAUCE:

1 tablespoon chopped oregano

300 ml/½ pint passata (sieved tomatoes)

½ teaspoon caster sugar

CHEESE SAUCE:

15 g/½ oz cornflour

300 ml/½ pint skimmed milk

50 g/2 oz low-fat Cheddar cheese, grated

1 To prepare the filling, remove any tough stalks from the spinach and put it into a large saucepan with just the water that clings to the leaves. Cook over a low heat for 5 minutes or until the leaves have wilted. Strain the spinach and squeeze out all the excess liquid. Chop the spinach finely and transfer it to a bowl.

2 Heat a large frying pan or wok and dry fry the onion for 3–6 minutes, stirring constantly, until soft. Add half of the onion to the spinach with the chicken, cheese and cinnamon, and season to taste. Stir well and spoon into the cannelloni tubes, then arrange them in a single layer in a rectangular 1.2 litre/2 pint ovenproof dish.

3 To make the tomato sauce, transfer the remaining onion to a saucepan and stir in the oregano, passata and sugar and simmer for 15 minutes.

4 To make the cheese sauce, mix the cornflour with a little milk, heat the remaining milk in a saucepan and then mix in the cornflour mixture. Simmer until thickened. Add the cheese and stir until melted.

5 Pour the tomato sauce over the filled cannelloni, followed by the cheese sauce. Sprinkle the grated cheese over the top. Bake in a preheated oven, 190°C (375°F), Gas Mark 5, for 45 minutes. Serve at once.

Serves 6

Preparation time: 20 minutes

Cooking time: 1¼ hours

Oven temperature: 190°C (375°F), Gas Mark 5

kcal 440; kJ 1864; Protein 29 (g); Fat 5 (g); CHO 73 (g)

Green Chilli Chicken with Spinach Taglioni

- 4 boneless, skinless chicken breasts, each about 75 g/3 oz
- 1 teaspoon olive oil
- 2 green chillies, deseeded and sliced
- 1 green pepper, cored, deseeded and sliced
- 1 teaspoon lime juice
- 1 x 400 g/13 oz can chopped tomatoes
- 15 g/½ oz pitted black olives
- 15 g/½ oz pitted green olives
- 250 g/8 oz dried spinach taglioni
- salt and pepper
- sprigs of flat leaf parsley, to garnish

1 Cut each chicken breast into 4 pieces. Heat a wok or large frying pan and add the oil; when it is hot, add the chicken pieces, chillies and green pepper. Stir-fry for about 5 minutes or until the chicken has browned.
2 Stir in the lime juice, tomatoes and olives, with salt and pepper to taste. Reduce the heat and simmer the sauce for 15 minutes.
3 Meanwhile, bring a large saucepan of water to the boil. Add the pasta, stir and cook for about 8–12 minutes, until *al dente*.
4 Drain the pasta. Pile it on to a large heated platter and spoon over the chicken mixture. Garnish with flat leaf parsley sprigs and serve at once.

Serve 4
Preparation time: 10 minutes
Cooking time: 20 minutes

kcal 335; kJ 1423; Protein 25 (g); Fat 5 (g); CHO 50 (g)

Chicken and Orange Shells

- 150 g/5 oz cooked chicken breast, roughly chopped
- grated rind of 1 orange
- 2 tablespoons orange juice
- 1 egg, separated
- 3 tablespoons very low-fat natural yogurt
- ½ teaspoon cayenne pepper
- 16 large dried pasta shells, cooked
- mixed salad leaves
- salt and pepper

1 Combine the chicken, orange rind, juice, egg yolk, yogurt and cayenne in a food processor. Add salt and pepper to taste and process for 1 minute or until smooth. Whisk the egg white in a grease-free bowl until firm peaks form then fold into the chicken mixture.
2 Spoon a little of the filling into each pasta shell. Arrange the shells in a steamer and steam for 15 minutes or until the chicken filling has set.
3 Arrange the salad leaves on four serving plates and place the shells on top and serve at once.

Serves 4
Preparation time: 10 minutes
Cooking time: 15 minutes

kcal 434; kJ 1841; Protein 26 (g); Fat 5 (g); CHO 76 (g)

Spaghetti alla Bolognese

- 500g/1 lb spaghetti
- 2 tablespoons Vegetable Stock (see page 8)
- 2 Spanish onions, chopped
- 1 tablespoon finely chopped rosemary
- 2 garlic cloves, crushed
- 2 x 400 g/13 oz cans chopped tomatoes
- 5 tablespoons tomato purée
- ½ teaspoon sugar
- 250 g/8 oz lean minced beef
- salt and pepper

1 Bring a large saucepan of salted water to the boil. Add the spaghetti, stir and cook for 10–12 minutes until *al dente*. Drain and season with pepper.
2 Meanwhile, heat the stock in a saucepan, add the onions and cook until soft. Add the rosemary and garlic and cook gently for 1 minute. Stir in the tomatoes, tomato purée, sugar and salt and pepper to taste. Simmer for 10–15 minutes. Mix in the beef and stir until browned. Gently bring back to the boil and simmer for 5 minutes. Serve at once, poured over the spaghetti.

Serves 4
Preparation time: 15 minutes
Cooking time: about 30 minutes

kcal 558; kJ 2371; Protein 31 (g); Fat 5 (g); CHO 103 (g)

Stir-fried Steak and Tagliatelle

- 1 garlic clove, crushed
- 1 teaspoon finely chopped fresh root ginger,
- 25 g/1 oz onion, finely chopped
- 200 g/7 oz steak, cut into very thin 4 cm/1½ inch strips
- 175 g/6 oz broccoli florets, finely sliced
- 125 g/4 oz mushrooms, finely sliced
- 2 tablespoons light soy sauce
- 4 tablespoons Vegetable Stock (see page 8)
- 1 teaspoon caster sugar
- 500 g/1 lb tagliatelle
- salt and pepper

1 Heat a large frying pan or wok over a moderate heat, add the garlic, ginger, onion and a pinch of salt and dry fry for 2–3 minutes, turning constantly.
2 Add the steak and stir-fry for 2–3 minutes, until brown on all sides.
3 Add the broccoli and continue to stir-fry for 2 minutes. Add the mushrooms, and soy sauce, stock and sugar and stir-fry for a further 3–4 minutes.
4 Meanwhile, bring a large saucepan of salted water to the boil. Add the pasta, stir and cook for 10–12 minutes until *al dente*. Drain the pasta, add to the wok and toss for a few more minutes to allow the pasta to absorb some of the juices. Add pepper to taste. Serve immediately.

Serves 4
Preparation time: 15–20 minutes
Cooking time: 15 minutes

kcal 518; kJ 22202; Protein 28 (g); Fat 5 (g); CHO 96 (g)

Coriander and Chive Meatballs

- 1 onion, grated
- 1 tablespoon freshly grated Parmesan cheese
- 150 g/5 oz lean minced beef
- 1 tablespoon tomato purée
- 1 teaspoon chilli sauce
- 1 bunch coriander, finely chopped
- 1 bunch chives, chopped
- 125 g/4 oz very finely chopped mushrooms
- 2 teaspoons sunflower oil
- 375 g/12 oz dried spaghetti
- salt and pepper
- sprigs of basil, to garnish

SAUCE:

- 1 onion, finely chopped
- 2 garlic cloves, crushed
- 1 x 400 g/13 oz can chopped tomatoes with herbs
- 2 tablespoons tomato purée
- 2 tablespoons chopped oregano

1 To make the meatballs, combine the onion, Parmesan, minced beef, tomato purée, chilli sauce, herbs and mushrooms in a bowl. Add salt and pepper and mix thoroughly.

2 Using dampened hands, shape the mixture into small balls. Heat the oil in a frying pan and fry the meatballs, in batches, for 10 minutes until browned. Using a slotted spoon, transfer the meatballs to a baking dish. Keep hot.

3 Bring a large pan of salted water to the boil. Add the pasta, stir and cook for 10–12 minutes, until *al dente*.

4 Meanwhile, make the sauce. Heat a wok or frying pan, add the onion and garlic and dry fry for 3–6 minutes, stirring constantly, until soft. Stir in the tomatoes, tomato purée and oregano. Simmer for 8 minutes.

5 Drain the pasta and pile it into a heated bowl. Pour over the sauce and toss lightly. Serve with the meatballs, garnished with basil sprigs.

Serves 6

Preparation time: 20 minutes
Cooking time: about 30 minutes

kcal 283; kJ 1197; Protein 14 (g); Fat 5 (g); CHO 48 (g)

Beef and Mangetout Stir-fry

- 25 g/1 oz fresh root ginger, shredded
- 1 garlic clove, crushed
- 4 tablespoons light soy sauce
- 2 tablespoons dry sherry
- 1 teaspoon chilli sauce
- 1 teaspoon clear honey
- ½ teaspoon Chinese five-spice powder
- 375 g/12 oz fillet steak, finely sliced
- 250 g/8 oz dried low-fat egg noodles
- 250 g/8 oz mangetout, trimmed
- salt and pepper
- shredded spring onions, to garnish

1 Combine the ginger, garlic, soy sauce, sherry, chilli sauce, honey and five-spice powder in a non-metallic bowl. Stir well. Add the steak, stir to coat thoroughly, then cover and marinate for at least 30 minutes.
2 Bring a large saucepan of lightly salted water to the boil. Add the noodles, remove the pan from the heat, cover and leave to stand for 5 minutes.
3 Meanwhile, heat a wok or frying pan. Add 2 tablespoons of the marinade and the beef and stir-fry for about 3–6 minutes.
4 Add the mangetout and the remaining marinade to the wok, with salt and pepper if required. Stir-fry for a further 2 minutes.
5 Drain the noodles and arrange them in warm serving bowls. Spoon the stir-fry over the top and garnish with shredded spring onions and serve.

Serves 4
Preparation time: 10 minutes, plus marinating and standing
Cooking time: 8 minutes

kcal 348; kJ 1475; Protein 27 (g); Fat 5 (g); CHO 50 (g)

Pasta
Salads

Pasta, Cucumber and Radish Salad

125 g/4 oz pasta shapes

175 g/6 oz radishes, sliced

½ cucumber, about 250 g/8 oz, unpeeled
and diced

150 ml/5 fl oz low-fat yogurt

1 cos lettuce

salt and pepper

2 finely chopped spring onions, to garnish

1 Bring a large saucepan of salted water to the boil. Add the pasta, stir and cook for
10–12 minutes until *al dente*. Rinse under cold running water and drain thoroughly.
2 Put the radishes and cucumber into a bowl and add the pasta.
3 Stir in the yogurt, season with plenty of pepper and a little salt. Toss the pasta,
radishes and cucumber in the yogurt to coat thoroughly.
4 Arrange the lettuce leaves on a serving dish and spoon the salad into them. Garnish
with the chopped spring onions.

Serves 4
Preparation time: 25 minutes
Cooking time: about 12 minutes

kcal 149; kJ 630; Protein 7 (g); Fat 1 (g); CHO 29 (g)

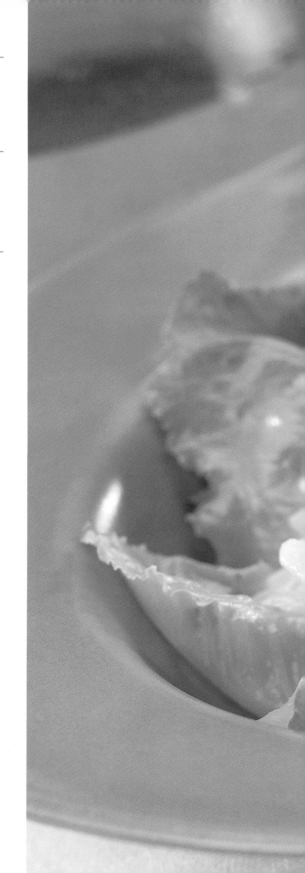

Pasta Twist Salad

- 125 g/4 oz wholewheat or plain pasta twists or shells
- 175 g/6 oz frozen sweetcorn kernels
- 4 celery sticks, sliced
- 4 tomatoes, skinned, quartered and seeded
- 4 spring onions, chopped
- 1 tablespoon parsley, to garnish
- celery leaves, to garnish

DRESSING:

- 1 x 150 g/5 oz carton natural low-fat yogurt
- 4 tablespoons tomato juice
- ¼ teaspoon Worcestershire sauce
- salt and pepper
- 2 teaspoons chopped oregano (optional)
- pinch of sugar

1 Bring a large saucepan of salted water to the boil. Add the pasta, stir and cook for 10–12 minutes until *al dente*. Drain and rinse under cold running water.

2 Meanwhile, cook the sweetcorn until tender in a saucepan of boiling water, following the packet instructions. Drain and leave to cool.

3 Mix together the pasta and sweetcorn with the celery, tomatoes and spring onions in a bowl.

4 Blend together all the dressing ingredients in a jug, then pour the dressing over the salad and toss well.

5 Spoon the salad into a serving dish and sprinkle with parsley. Cover and chill for about 30 minutes before serving garnished with celery leaves.

Serves 6

Preparation time: 15 minutes, plus chilling
Cooking time: about 30 minutes

kcal 134; kJ 571; Protein 5 (g); Fat 1 (g); CHO 28 (g)

Italian Pasta Salad

Crunchy baby corn cobs make this pasta salad extra special and the apple in the dressing gives it a tangy, piquant flavour.

- 250 g/8 oz small pasta shapes
- 1 teaspoon vegetable oil
- 175 g/6 oz baby corn cobs
- 125 g/4 oz raisins
- 1 red pepper, cored, deseeded and sliced
- chopped chives, to garnish

DRESSING:

- 3 tablespoons low-fat mayonnaise
- 3 tablespoons unsweetened apple purée
- 2 tablespoons snipped chives
- salt and pepper

1 Bring a large saucepan of salted water to the boil. Add the pasta and oil, stir and cook for 10–12 minutes until *al dente*. Drain and cool under cold water. Drain again thoroughly.
2 Meanwhile, cook the baby corn cobs in boiling salted water for 5 minutes or until tender but still crisp. Drain well.
3 Mix the pasta with the baby corn, raisins and pepper in a serving bowl.
4 To make the dressing, mix the mayonnaise with the apple purée, chives and salt and pepper to taste. Fold into the pasta mixture and mix. Garnish with chives.

Serves 6
Preparation time: 10 minutes
Cooking time: 15 minutes

kcal 243; kJ 1030; Protein 7 (g); Fat 4 (g); CHO 49 (g)

Pasta Slaw

- 75 g/3 oz pasta spirals (fusilli)
- 300 g/10 oz French beans
- 75 g/3 oz white cabbage, roughly chopped
- 1 carrot, grated
- 4 spring onions, finely chopped
- salt and pepper
- parsley sprigs, to garnish (optional)

DRESSING:

- 4 tablespoons low-fat mayonnaise
- 2 tablespoons skimmed milk
- 1 tablespoon balsamic or wine vinegar
- 2 teaspoons sugar
- salt and pepper

1 Bring a saucepan of salted water to the boil. Add the pasta, stir and cook for 10–12 minutes until *al dente*. At the same time, bring a second pan of salted water to the boil and cook the French beans for 3–5 minutes. Refresh the pasta and beans under cold running water, drain and leave to cool.
2 Meanwhile, mix together the remaining salad ingredients in a bowl. Combine the ingredients for the dressing in a jug and add to the salad bowl with the pasta and French beans. Season to taste and garnish with parsley sprigs, if using, and serve.

Serves 4
Preparation time: 15 minutes, plus cooling
Cooking time: 10–12 minutes

kcal 146; kJ 612; Protein 5 (g); Fat 5 (g); CHO 22 (g)

Wholewheat Pasta Salad

- 250 g/8 oz wholewheat pasta twists (fusilli)
- 100 ml/3½ fl oz fresh orange juice
- 2 tablespoons fresh lime juice
- 1 tablespoon fresh lemon juice
- 1 teaspoon cider vinegar
- ½ teaspoon granular low-calorie sweetener
- 2 spring onions, chopped
- 125 g/4 oz French beans, cooked
- 4 tomatoes, skinned, quartered and seeded
- 50 g/2 oz pitted black olives, to garnish
- salt and pepper

1 Bring a large saucepan of salted water to the boil. Add the pasta, stir and cook for 10–12 minutes until *al dente*. Drain well.

2 Mix the orange, lime and lemon juices, vinegar and sweetener together in a bowl. Season with pepper and pour over the hot pasta. Mix well together, cover and leave until cold.

3 Stir the spring onions, beans and tomatoes into the pasta and mix well with the dressing. To serve, turn into a large salad bowl and scatter over the black olives.

Serves 4

Preparation time: 10–12 minutes, plus cooling
Cooking time: 12 minutes

kcal 245; kJ 1040; Protein 10 (g); Fat 3 (g); CHO 47 (g)

Fennel and Pasta Salad

• 500 g/1 lb dried pasta shells or bows
• 3 large fennel bulbs, sliced, leaves reserved for garnish
• 2–3 red dessert apples, cored and sliced
• juice of 1 lemon
• 4 shallots, chopped
• 4 tomatoes, skinned and chopped

DRESSING:

• 3 teaspoons olive oil
• 2 tablespoons lemon juice
• 1 teaspoon French mustard
• 1 teaspoon honey
• 1 tablespoon each chopped parsley and basil

1 Bring a large saucepan of salted water to the boil. Add the pasta, stir and cook for 10–12 minutes until *al dente*. Drain and cool quickly under cold running water. Drain thoroughly and place in a large bowl.
2 Toss the fennel and apples in the lemon juice, then add to the pasta with the shallots and tomatoes.
3 Mix the dressing ingredients together and pour over the salad. Transfer to a serving bowl and garnish with the fennel leaves. Serve immediately.

Serves 4
Preparation time: 15 minutes, plus cooling
Cooking time: 10–12 minutes

kcal 497; kJ 2114; Protein 17 (g); Fat 5 (g); CHO 103 (g)

Tagliatelle Riviera

A delicious accompaniment to this dish is a fresh rocket and basil salad lightly tossed with low-fat vinaigrette.

- **2 teaspoons olive oil**
- **2 onions, sliced**
- **2 garlic cloves, crushed**
- **2 slices lean bacon, derinded and chopped**
- **250 g/8 oz mushrooms, sliced**
- **2 anchovy fillets, chopped**
- **6 pitted black olives, halved**
- **500 g/1 lb tagliatelle**
- **1 tablespoon freshly grated Parmesan cheese**
- **salt and pepper**

1 Heat the oil in a frying pan. Add the onions, garlic and bacon and fry until the onions are soft but not brown. Stir in the mushrooms, anchovy fillets, olives and salt and pepper to taste. Cook for a further 4–5 minutes or until very hot.

2 Meanwhile, bring a large saucepan of salted water to the boil. Add the pasta, stir and cook for 10–12 minutes until *al dente*. Drain the tagliatelle and arrange in a warm bowls. To serve, spoon over the sauce and sprinkle with the Parmesan.

Serves 4

Preparation time: 10 minutes
Cooking time: about 20 minutes

kcal 478; kJ 2030; Protein 18 (g); Fat 5 (g); CHO 95 (g)

Tagliatelle Salad

- 500 g/1 lb fresh tagliatelle verde
- 2 x 425 g/14 oz cans red kidney beans, rinsed and drained
- 2 x 200 g/7 oz cans tuna in brine, drained and flaked
- 4 courgettes, thinly sliced
- 50 g/2 oz mushrooms, thinly sliced
- 2 shallots, chopped
- 1 tablespoon green peppercorns
- cayenne pepper
- salt

DRESSING:
- 4 tablespoons low-fat natural yogurt
- 2 tablespoons chopped parsley
- 2 tablespoons chopped chives
- 2 teaspoons lemon juice
- 1 teaspoon finely grated lemon rind

TO GARNISH:
- mint sprigs (optional)
- lemon wedges

1 Bring a large saucepan of salted water to the boil. Add the pasta, stir and cook for 4–5 minutes until *al dente*. Drain and cool quickly under cold running water. Drain thoroughly and place in a large bowl.

2 Add the kidney beans, tuna, courgettes, mushrooms and shallots to the pasta along with the peppercorns. Mix together well.

3 Mix all the dressing ingredients together, and season with cayenne pepper and salt to taste. Fold the dressing into the salad and transfer to a large serving bowl.

4 Garnish with mint sprigs, if using, and lemon wedges. Serve immediately.

Serves 6

Preparation time: 15 minutes
Cooking time: 5 minutes

kcal 500; kJ 2129; Protein 39 (g); Fat 4 (g); CHO 84 (g)

Herring and Apple Salad

- 125 g/4 oz large pasta shells
- 150 g/5 oz low-fat natural yogurt
- 2 tablespoons raisins
- 2 red dessert apples, cored and thinly sliced
- grated rind and juice of ½ lemon
- 1 tablespoon chopped parsley
- 2 small rollmops, about 100–150 g/4–5 oz, cut into pieces
- salt and pepper

1 Bring a large saucepan of salted water to the boil. Add the pasta, stir and cook for 10–12 minutes until *al dente*. Rinse and drain. While warm, mix the pasta with a little diluted yogurt and stir in the raisins and apples.
2 Mix the remaining yogurt with the lemon rind and juice, and the parsley and season to taste.
3 Place the pasta on a shallow serving dish and arrange the rollmops on top. Spoon over the sauce and serve.

Serves 4
Preparation time: 10 minutes
Cooking time: about 12 minutes

kcal 248; kJ 1049; Protein 13 (g); Fat 5 (g); CHO 40 (g)

Country Salad

- 250 g/8 oz rigatoni or penne
- 2 teaspoons olive oil
- 4 tomatoes, skinned and chopped
- 1 green pepper, cored, deseeded and chopped
- 50 g/2 oz stuffed olives, sliced
- 175 g/6 oz button mushrooms, sliced
- 1 tablespoon tomato ketchup
- 6 tablespoons very low-fat yogurt
- juice of ½ lemon
- salt and pepper
- lettuce leaves, to serve

1 Bring a large saucepan of salted water to the boil. Add the pasta, stir and cook for 10–12 minutes until *al dente*. Drain well and mix with the oil, then leave to cool.

2 Mix the tomatoes, green pepper, olives and mushrooms into the pasta and season with salt and pepper. Mix the tomato ketchup with the yogurt and lemon juice, and stir into the salad until evenly coated. Serve on a bed of lettuce leaves.

Serves 4

Preparation time: 15 minutes, plus cooling
Cooking time: about 12 minutes

kcal 276; kJ 1170; Protein 10 (g); Fat 5 (g); CHO 52 (g)

Winter Salad

- 175 g/6 oz pasta bows
- 175 g/6 oz cooked, skinless chicken, diced
- 2 celery sticks, diced
- 2 red dessert apples, cored and diced
- 1 green pepper, cored, deseeded and diced
- 4 tablespoons low-fat mayonnaise
- salt and pepper
- ½ head lettuce, to serve

1 Bring a large saucepan of salted water to the boil. Add the pasta bows, stir and cook for 10–12 minutes until *al dente*. Drain well and leave to cool.
2 Mix the chicken with the celery, apples, green pepper and pasta bows and season to taste with salt and pepper. Fold in the mayonnaise, turn into a salad bowl and serve with the lettuce, some of which could be shredded, if you like.

Serves 6
Preparation time: 15 minutes, plus cooling
Cooking time: about 12 minutes

kcal 192; kJ 809; Protein 13 (g); Fat 5 (g); CHO 26 (g)

Provençal Pasta Salad

- 175 g/6 oz rigatoni or penne
- 4 tablespoons low-fat mayonnaise
- juice of ½ lemon
- 6 tomatoes, skinned, deseeded and chopped
- 125 g/4 oz French beans, cooked
- 12 black olives, pitted
- 1 x 200 g/7 oz can tuna in brine, drained and flaked
- salt and pepper
- 1 small head lettuce, shredded, to serve
- 1 x 50 g/2 oz can anchovy fillets, drained and washed, to garnish

1 Bring a large saucepan of salted water to the boil. Add the pasta, stir and cook for 10–12 minutes until *al dente*. Drain the pasta well and mix with a little of the dressing.

2 When the pasta is cool, turn it into a bowl and mix with the tomatoes, beans, olives, flaked tuna and season with salt and pepper.

2 Toss the salad lightly in the remaining dressing and serve on a bed of shredded lettuce and garnished with anchovies.

Serves 6
Preparation time: 10–12 minutes, plus cooling
Cooking time: about 12 minutes

kcal 198; kJ 839; Protein 14 (g); Fat 5 (g); CHO 26 (g)

Courgette and Pasta Salad

- 175 g/6 oz pasta shells
- 3 tablespoons low-fat mayonnaise diluted with 1 tablespoon tomato juice
- 4 courgettes, sliced
- 2 tomatoes, skinned and chopped
- 8 pitted black olives
- 2 spring onions, chopped
- 1 tablespoon chopped parsley
- salt and pepper

1 Bring a large saucepan of salted water to the boil. Add the pasta, stir and cook for 10–12 minutes until *al dente*. Rinse and drain well. While still warm, mix the pasta with the dressing.
2 Meanwhile, cook the courgettes in boiling salted water for 8 minutes until just tender, then drain and cool. Add to the pasta with the tomatoes, olives, spring onions and parsley and season with salt and pepper. Mix well and serve cold.

Serves 4
Preparation time: 10 minutes, plus cooling
Cooking time: 10–12 minutes

kcal 213; kJ 900; Protein 7 (g); Fat 5 (g); CHO 37 (g)

Italian Salmon Salad

- 175 g/6 oz pasta bows
- 1 x 200 g/7 oz can salmon in brine, drained and flaked
- 1 red pepper, cored, deseeded and finely diced
- ½ cucumber, finely diced
- 10 pitted black olives
- 2 tablespoons low-fat mayonnaise
- sprigs of watercress, to garnish

1 Bring a large saucepan of salted water to the boil. Add the pasta, stir and cook for 10–12 minutes until *al dente*. Drain thoroughly and leave to cool.

2 Mix the flaked salmon with the red pepper, cucumber, olives and pasta. Pour over the low-fat mayonnaise and toss lightly. Arrange in a serving dish and garnish with watercress sprigs.

Serves 6

Preparation time: 15 minutes, plus cooling
Cooking time: 10–12 minutes

kcal 180; kJ 758; Protein 11 (g); Fat 5 (g); CHO 24 (g)

Melon and Prawn Cocktail

- 125 g/4 oz pasta spirals
- 2 tomatoes, skinned and cut into 8 pieces
- ½ honeydew melon, cubed
- 175 g/6 oz cooked peeled prawns
- ½ cucumber, cubed

½ teaspoon cayenne pepper

DRESSING:

- 3 tablespoons low-fat mayonnaise
- 1 tablespoon tomato ketchup
- 3 tablespoons low-fat natural yogurt
- salt and pepper

1 Bring a large saucepan of salted water to the boil. Add the pasta, stir and cook for 10–12 minutes until *al dente*. Rinse and drain well.

2 Mix the pasta, tomatoes, melon, prawns and cucumber together in a bowl. Make the dressing by mixing the mayonnaise, tomato ketchup, and yogurt and season with salt and pepper. Pour the dressing over the pasta mixture and toss well. To serve, spoon into glasses and sprinkle each with a little cayenne pepper.

Serves 4
Preparation time: 15 minutes
Cooking time: 10–12 minutes

kcal 225; kJ 947; Protein 15 (g); Fat 5 (g); CHO 32 (g)

Penne Primavera

Other vegetables that would be delicious in Penne Primavera include fennel, mushrooms, fresh peas, cauliflower, asparagus or red pepper.

- 125 g/4 oz broccoli, broken into small pieces
- 125 g/4 oz French beans, cut into 5 cm/2 inch lengths
- 125 g/4 oz mangetout
- 2 tablespoons chopped herbs
- 500 g/1 lb penne

VINAIGRETTE:

- 3 teaspoons olive oil
- 2 tablespoons cider or wine vinegar
- 2 teaspoons French mustard or 1 teaspoon English mustard
- 1 teaspoon caster sugar
- freshly grated nutmeg (optional)
- 1 garlic clove, crushed (optional)
- salt and pepper

1 Steam the vegetables for 2–4 minutes until slightly softened but still brightly coloured and crisp. Drain, and put into a large bowl.
2 To make the vinaigrette, blend together all the ingredients and pour over the vegetables. Sprinkle the vegetables with the herbs.
3 Meanwhile, bring a large saucepan of salted water to the boil. Add the pasta, stir and cook for 10–12 minutes until *al dente*. Drain, and mix into the bowl of vegetables and vinaigrette. Serve hot or cold.

Serves 4
Preparation time: 20 minutes
Cooking time: 15 minutes

kcal 476; kJ 2021; Protein 18 (g); Fat 5 (g); CHO 96 (g)

Recipe photographers:
Reed Consumer Books Ltd.
Clive Streeter, and Trevor Wood
Special Photography:
Simon Smith

Jacket photography
by Simon Smith
Jacket Home Economists:
Lucy Knox and Sarah Lowman